The Words That Went Unspoken

Walking Through Denial, Faith, and Loss

Ellie Sager Mercer

with Elizabeth Peavey

If you bring forth that which is within you, it will save you.
If you do not bring it forth, it will destroy you.

from the Gospel of Thomas

PALMETTO
PUBLISHING

Charleston, SC
www.PalmettoPublishing.com

The Words That Went Unspoken

Copyright © 2021 by Ellie Sager Mercer

First Edition

Paperback: 978-1-64990-871-1
eBook: 978-1-64990-872-8

In memory of Berta, Jeannie and Perry

Introduction

Beep. Beep. Beep. I can hear the monitors measuring Perry's blood pressure as I peek through the open door to her room in the intensive care unit at Cedars-Sinai Medical Center. It's July 2010, my third trip to Los Angeles from Maine in six months. I'm already exhausted. Green, red, and blue lights flash on the screen beside her. She's attached to bags of fluids dripping into her veins. My sister is dying.

My niece rushes over, gives me a hug, and says, "Auntie, thank you for coming!" Rachael is a brand-new mother who is, at the same time, losing her own mother. Her eyes fill with tears as she closes the heavy glass door to the room so we can have privacy. Perry is sleeping soundly for the first time in days. Too many doctors. So many different opinions. They say they have never seen anything like this. This cancer has spread faster than any of them would have predicted. Perry is so tired, so weak, not eating, drinking, or talking. I try to hide my shock.

Rachael returns home hours later to be with her husband and new baby. I fall into a deep sleep in the recliner beside Perry's bed. At two a.m. I am woken by the sound of voices. My eyes slowly adjust to the light in the room as I take in the scene by my sister's bedside. Something is wrong.

A doctor is speaking with her. I am alert enough to notice that he is young, probably the same age as my two sons. I like his voice. It's calm and reassuring. He explains to Perry that he's going to insert a line in her foot with medicine to raise her blood pressure. I sit up. She asks, "Is this going to hurt?"

"I can't promise it won't," he replies.

Perry looks him in the eye. "If you hurt me, I'll pierce your ears."

"Don't worry," he says with a smile, "This isn't an unusual procedure."

Her wit disarms him. It catches him off guard. That's why he comes in the middle of the night. That's why he does the procedure himself rather than leaving it to whoever is on call. My sister can turn any conversation into a *Tonight Show* monologue.

His skilled hands never stop working as he inserts an intravenous line in her ankle in order to get more fluids into her. He makes it look so easy, like threading a needle. This must not be such a big deal, I tell myself. He has clearly performed this procedure thousands of times. When he finally leaves, it's almost dawn.

Perry and I are able to get a couple more hours of sleep before the medical whirlwind that is her care begins: the blood pressure checks, the neurological assessments, the cardiac evaluations, the pulmonary examinations. She is the focus of several specialists. They compare notes, attempting to create a plan of care. I have the sense they are in uncharted territory.

Carla, the day nurse, comes bustling in fresh from a good night's sleep to check the monitors. I squint as she pulls back the curtain and flicks on the light. She mentions that the late-night visit from the doctor was unusual. He is one of the best neurosurgeons in the country and will be overseeing her care. She tells me a procedure like the one he performed would typically be left to an on-call physician. I wonder if my sister is getting preferential treatment because her son has connections. I don't care about the reason why. I'm just glad she is in such capable hands.

A CNA places a breakfast tray in front of Perry, but she pushes it away. I look at it longingly. I haven't had anything substantial to eat for twenty-four hours. Would it be totally out of line for me to eat the eggs and that overdone wheat toast?

I can tell the blood pressure is still not where they want it to be, because Carla hauls out her manual blood pressure cuff to see if she can get a different reading. It feels so routine, so matter-of-fact as she rips at the Velcro to remove the cuff. "Here, let me fluff your pillows for you," she clucks to my sister. She's too cheerful for me. I want to say, *You do know my sister is dying. Right?*

A specialist comes in to assess whether Perry's elevated white blood cell count is an infection or an indication that the cancer has spread. Next a phlebotomist arrives to draw more blood. Perry is then taken for more scans to try and determine the cause. The results are clear: It's the cancer. The day continues with a flurry of white coats in and out of her room. I start sinking into the reality of her prognosis. I want to hold out hope that this cancer can be treated.

But I know how this is going to end. I've been here before.

Chapter 1

Since childhood, I've been afraid of the dark. It wasn't the scary-monster kind of dark that frightened me, but the fear-of-abandonment kind of dark. If I closed my eyes, I could sometimes imagine I was floating all alone in space. That cold nothingness terrified me.

In one of the earliest dreams I can remember, I was walking with my father to the Philips Building, the main building on campus, to get the mail. While we were there, he began talking with a friend and forgot that I was with him. He left without me. Night was falling, and I didn't know how to get home.

Of course, that dream was silly. My father, Art Sager, was my great protector. He was a teacher at Governor Dummer Academy, now the Governor's Academy, in South Byfield, Massachusetts. Founded in 1763 on 460 acres of farmland, it is the oldest continuously operating boarding school in America. Until the mid-1970s, Governor Dummer was an all-boys academy. In addition to his teaching duties, my father coached football and track, was in charge of the music program, and, like all the other "masters," was responsible for dormitory life for the forty junior and senior high school boys in the dorm. I thought he was the most important man in the world.

We lived in an apartment at the end of that boy-filled dorm. World War II had ended two years before, but the windows in our home still had green blackout shades that were reminders of the threat of German invasion. There were practice air raid drills at the four-room elementary school I attended. When the fire department blared its siren, we scrambled out of our chairs and squeezed under our desks. I sat in the back row and would look out the window next to my desk and wait for the bombs to fall. Each time I heard the sirens, I feared we all were going to die.

One morning, I walked out the front door of our home and plunked myself down on a patch of green grass at the top of a small hill where I would go when I wanted to be alone. I was six and a half. The June sun was bright, and I was shaded by the leaves of a towering elm tree. To my right was a classroom building with a cupola that housed a large bronze bell. Every forty minutes, one of the students would ring the bell signaling the end of one class and the beginning of another. Even though I was reassured by its predictable tolling, I began to feel a pit grow in my stomach. This was the last day of classes for the school year, and the bell would not ring again until September, when the students returned.

Well, not all of them.

I had a crush on one of the seniors. His name was Tom. Tom had brown curly hair and called me "Slug," a nickname given to me by one of the seniors when I was three as I was riding my tricycle slowly down a path outside the dorm. I thought I was going to marry Tom when I grew up. But suddenly a thought exploded in my mind: *Tom is graduating. That means he's not coming back. Ever.* If Tom could suddenly disappear from my life, what did that mean about everyone else? What if something happened to my parents? To my sister, Jeannie? What if I could no longer hear my mother's voice or my father's laughter? It's not that I didn't know about death. I did. Jeannie's cat, Judy, had died the previous fall, and we buried her in the woods near our house. But the thought of something happening to my parents or Jeannie was different.

From my hilltop perch, I could hear my mother in the kitchen only a few feet away singing, "Glow, little glow worm, glimmer, glimmer," a hit song from her teen years. I liked listening to the sound of her voice as she went through her daily chores of dusting, carpet sweeping, and cooking. When she finished, I knew she would fix lunch for Jeannie and me. Then she would shed her apron, lie down for a ten-minute nap, get up, and change out of her "morning dress" into a suit with a silk blouse and pearls. Usually, I felt comforted by her routine. But today, it didn't take away my fear about what it would be like if something happened to my family.

The previous night, I'd woken up from a nightmare. The room was pitch-black. A bear was under my bed. I tried to call out, "Daddy, Mommy...HELP!" but no sound came out. My vocal cords wouldn't work. I was alone with a bear and my terror. I wondered if this was what death was like, being scared and alone in a dark emptiness.

As the bell rang, I watched the boys walk out of the classroom building toward the dining hall for lunch. My mother's voice now seemed very far away. I felt so alone on my hill. I could feel tears forming. I decided to think about God. In church, I had heard big words like *crucifixion* and *resurrection*. I didn't know what they meant, but they had something to do with dying and coming back to life. We learned there was this man called Jesus who did that. If *he* did it then probably the rest of us could, which gave me hope. And then I heard my mother call me. "Eleanor, come get your lunch."

I dried my tears and walked back toward the house. As I got closer, the aroma of freshly baked chocolate chip cookies drifted in my direction. I let the screen door bang behind me. I never wanted to be very far away from my mother. I was with her now and everything was OK.

Hanging on a wall outside the kitchen was a picture of her sitting in a chair holding me when I was a baby. Jeannie, four years older than me, was standing beside her. I loved looking at her beautiful profile, her short dark hair, her high cheekbones, and the way she gazed at me.

Soon she was going to have another baby. I knew the time was getting close because she had been making casseroles, custards, and puddings to last us for the few days she would be in the hospital. The crib had been set up in our parents' bedroom, and Jeannie and I were getting ready by making sure our new sister or brother had enough toys. We gathered stuffed animals from our own beds and placed them along the side rails of the crib. In a room off the kitchen, I could hear the whir of a sewing machine as my grandmother put the finishing touches on a cloth clown doll. If the baby was a boy, his name would be Andrew. If it was a girl, her name would be Ann Perry.

As I sat at the table, I had an urge to tell my mother everything I'd been thinking. But I was too embarrassed to let her know how much I loved Tom. I didn't want her to know that thinking about death and dying scared me. I didn't tell her I imagined being alone in an endless void that extended forever in time and space. And I couldn't tell her my dream about the bear. I didn't share my fears with her or with anyone else because whenever I tried to talk about them, I would be told I was just a worrier, like Eeyore with his tail between his legs. I finished my lunch, pushed my thoughts about life and death aside, and went to join my grandmother and her sewing.

Very early in the morning on June 17th, my father took my mother to the hospital. Jeannie and I tried to busy ourselves while we waited at home. After several hours, the phone rang. My father, who had returned to wait with us, called out, "It's a girl!"

Another girl on an all-boys campus! We climbed into my father's 1945 DeSoto and raced to the hospital. Because children under 12 were not allowed in the maternity ward, Jeannie and I had to stand outside in the parking lot and wait for our mother to come to her window on the second floor. It seemed like forever before she finally appeared holding Ann Perry, soon to be just Perry. It was our first glimpse at who was to become our unconventional, outrageously funny little sister. Wrapped in a baby blanket in our mother's arms, we gave her the name "Precie" right then and there. Short for Precious.

We lived in an idyllic place. Behind our house, there were thick woods where we built forts and a cranberry bog where we skated in winter. In summer, we picked blueberries in a high-bush patch. We punched holes in pails, tied string through them, and hung them around our necks. The sound of *plink-plink* was a giveaway that some of us were eating the harvest rather than collecting them for pies and muffins. There were athletic fields, hockey rinks, and two gyms. When the boys left for the summer, we had entire dormitories in which to play hide-and-seek and classrooms with blackboards where we played school. I couldn't imagine how anyone lived in a town. What would there be to do?

Governor Dummer was a place of privilege. I thought we were wealthy like most of the students. My father was paid $3,000 a year when he joined the faculty in 1930, not long after the start of the Great Depression. He was thrilled to have a place to live and to be earning anything at all. At the height of his teaching and coaching career, in 1967, his annual income was $7,000.

In the nearby rural town where Jeannie and I went to grammar school, people were not as fortunate as we were. Many of the children came from poor families. When my mother heard that a girl in my grade only owned three dresses, she provided hand-me-down clothes for her. The only industry was a snuff mill, where men who were lucky enough to be employed worked. I remember the school nurse coming into each of the four classrooms every week to check for head lice. No one would have considered performing such a function on the children of Governor Dummer faculty.

I was always curious about what life was like for my mother when she was my age, but she didn't talk much about her past. Her mother had come from England and was orphaned shortly after she arrived in this country. Her father was the treasurer of one of two lucrative family-owned New England fiber mills, but I knew very little about the mills or her family. My mother's younger brother used to tell my sisters and me that the reason my grandfather married my grandmother was so he could sleep with her.

Every once in a while, my mother would laugh and remind us that she was the valedictorian of her high school class, and the boy who was the salutatorian became the Under Secretary of the Treasury in the Eisenhower Administration in the 1950s. That was the extent of her sense of self-importance, but that story profiled who she was: smart with a soft and gentle heart. The quote beside her senior picture in the Mt. Holyoke yearbook read: "She does not need to be ostentatious to hold responsible positions; she needs no raucous expletives to improve her gentle humor; she does not need to be collegiate to be universally liked."

She preferred staying at home. She ordered groceries over the phone and had them delivered. Large social gatherings were a challenge for her, but she capably performed the obligatory functions attached to a faculty wife in a private school in those days. She served tea after athletic events and hosted faculty coffees two or three times a year. Eventually she was invited to join the faculty, teaching French. She dedicated herself to the work: preparing classes, correcting tests and homework, and spending one-on-one time with students. It suited her reserved nature.

My father, on the other hand, was delighted to talk about his childhood. An accomplished athlete who threw the javelin in the 1928 Olympics in Amsterdam, he came from humble beginnings in a tight-knit family in Gardiner, Maine. "My father," he told me, "worked as a grocer six days a week, from seven a.m. to six p.m. One week's pay was eighteen dollars." He smiled and said, "We never felt like we didn't have enough. Our house was always filled with people and fun and laughter. My parents were like magnets. Everyone wanted to be around them." He described how, every Sunday afternoon, the whole family gathered around the old upright piano, played instruments, and sang. "No one had lessons," he said, "we just improvised." He played the trombone without being able to read music, and his sister played the piano for the silent movies. One of his favorite stories was about the time she was playing "Hail, Hail, the Gang's All Here," and she looked up at the movie screen to see a funeral procession. As untrained as he was, my father had enough talent to spend much of his life responsible for the music program at Governor Dummer.

When my father walked into a room, people noticed. I never met anyone who didn't love him. He was the one who encouraged me to try athletics in spite of my asthma, bought me a violin when I expressed an interest in music, took me to hear string quartets, and ensured that I visited the Hayden Planetarium in New York City to share his interest in the stars. I often had severe asthma attacks, the kind that kept me up all night trying to catch my next breath. My father would hear me coughing and fighting to breathe. I always knew he'd appear. If I didn't improve, he'd take me for a drive, hoping that a change in air would help. He made me feel safe.

My mother made me feel safe in a different way. She read to us every night. She took us to the library. I roamed through the stacks and could choose three books to take home. I read *Lassie Come Home* five times.

Each week she and I boarded a train to Boston for my appointment with an allergist. While we sat in the waiting room, my mother read aloud poems from *When We Were Very Young* by A.A. Milne, or sometimes chapters from *Winnie the Pooh*. "James James Morrison Morrison Weatherby George Dupree" was supposed to take my mind off the five shots about to be shoved into my arms with needles that looked like spears. The coarse texture of the paper, the musty-book smell, the black-and-white illustrations managed to be a distraction until the dreaded moment arrived when I heard my name called. "Eleanor?" The nurse would look at me with a smile. She knew me well. Dr. McMacken would cheerfully invite me to hop up on the examining table as he took a seat across from my mother.

"So, how's your husband's football team doing, Mrs. Sager?" He played with the syringes, pushing the vial filled with serum in and out while I sat quietly, my legs dangling from the table. The waiting was agony. Finally, he would look at me and say, "OK, Eleanor, time to roll up your sleeves." My mother held out her hands so I could I squeeze them when he made the attack. I turned my head the other way, so I didn't have to look. A dab of alcohol, and then he jabbed the needles into my arms. One syringe at a time; three shots in one arm and two in the other.

As a treat for enduring my shots, my mother would take me out for a special lunch at Shraft's Restaurant. It was big and fancy with white tablecloths and had an indoor balcony where I liked to sit. My grandmother, who lived in an apartment in Boston, would meet us there. I always ordered an egg salad sandwich with tomato aspic salad and a chocolate milkshake. My mother and my grandmother seemed to have a lot to say to each other that didn't include me. But that was OK. I felt secure just being with them.

Sometimes when I had nothing else to do, I'd ride my bike down what we called "the back road"—a country road that wound through a saltwater marsh dotted with rounded haystacks placed on wooden stilts. It led to Thurlow's Bridge, a rickety wooden structure suspended over the Parker River, which had dangerous whirlpools. One time, a boy from my grammar school dove in, got trapped in one, and drowned. If you walked across the bridge, you could see the roiling river through the slats. I was afraid that I would fall through them and be swallowed up by the current, like he was, so I never rode across it.

Looking back from the bridge, I could see a sliver of a house hidden by thick trees. I would straddle my bike and stare, leaning right and left over the handlebars so I could inspect it more carefully. *That has to be a castle in there!* But no matter which way I leaned, I never caught more than a partial view. I could see a turret—just like the one where Rapunzel let down her hair. Every time I rode down that road, I'd peer through the trees, straining to catch a glimpse of the house. It looked like a place where secrets were held, and I wanted to know what they were. If only I could get a closer look. I'd get back on my bike and ride as far as the entrance to the path that led to the castle. A sign blocking it had big black letters that said "No Trespassing. Police Take Notice." I would stare at the words, wanting to ignore them and walk down the path into the woods. But then I imagined the sound of sirens and an approaching police car. I saw myself being handcuffed, arrested, and put in jail. However, I knew that someday I had to go there. It looked like a place where secrets were kept, and I wanted to know what they were. But I never dared to disobey the signs. I didn't have the courage.

Chapter 2

Jeannie and I attended Sunday school at the nearby Episcopal Church, where my father was the choir director. The children's service consisted of worship with a children's choir. When the vestry doors opened, I felt like I was part of a royal procession, in my red satin robe. We followed a deep red carpet into the sanctuary, singing "Joyful, Joyful, We Adore Thee." Filing into the chancel, we took our seats in the choir loft and settled in as the Reverend Daniel Boone—a direct descendant of the famous frontiersman—offered the morning's liturgy. A mystery filled the space. It smelled of seasoned dark wood, and lilies or roses, or other fresh flowers on the altar. Light filtered through stained-glass windows, imbuing the sanctuary with a sense of warmth. The minister wore stoles of different colors. I liked the purple one best, but it seemed he didn't wear that often. Sunday after Sunday, we heard the same creed until we knew it by heart:

I believe in God, the Father Almighty,
the Maker of heaven and earth,
and in Jesus Christ, His only Son, our Lord.
Who was conceived by the Holy Ghost,

born of the Virgin Mary,
suffered under Pontius Pilate,
was crucified, died and was buried.
He descended into Hell
The third day he rose again…

I took this literally. God was an old man with a white beard who lived in the sky. I wasn't sure how Jesus could be his son, but I figured I'd better accept what I was told. I was afraid to ask questions because I was afraid to admit I didn't understand any of it.

When our service was over, we shed our robes and took our places in the pews where each class had a designated spot. The teacher read stories from the Bible, said prayers, and handed out worksheets with questions for us to think about. Some of the stories were hard to believe. For example, this man Jesus changed water into wine and fed 5,000 people with three fish and a few loaves of bread. He also made blind men see and dead people come alive. I wondered, *Could any of us do that?* but I didn't ask; our job was to be still and listen. My gaze would wander over to the windows, where the glass figures looked like hard candy. None appeared too friendly, but at least they were colorful. I wondered why there were so many halos, and who got to wear them, and why.

My mother sometimes attended church with us, but when I was ten, she decided to leave the Episcopal Church and join the Christian Science church. Neither my mother nor my father discussed this with my sisters and me. They just decided that Jeannie, Perry, and I would join her at this new church.

There was no priest or minister. There was no choir, no red carpet, no procession of singing children in satin robes, no ceremony or ritual at all. There were no stained-glass windows, no smell of old wood or fresh flowers, no warmth or feeling of mystery. Just two lecterns at the front of a whitewashed sanctuary. A woman wearing a floor-length dress that swished when she walked would appear from a side door and take her place at one lectern; a man in a dark suit would appear from the opposite door and stand at the other one. The man, known as the First Reader, would read from the Bible. The woman, known as the Second Reader, would read from *Science and Health with Key to the Scriptures* by Mary Baker Eddy, the founder of Christian Science.

Sometimes children were invited to the adult service, but mostly we attended Sunday school in the building next door. The classrooms were painted beige and furnished with straight-back chairs and metal tables. We sat at attention while a teacher explained the writings of Mary Baker Eddy. We were taught that if we focused our thoughts on God's power to heal, we would not need doctors. So why did I still have asthma? I guess I wasn't doing it right. Engraved on a panel in the front of the church was a quote from the Bible: "Be ye therefore perfect even as your Father in heaven is perfect." If that meant perfect behavior, I might qualify, but if it meant perfect health, then I had already missed the mark. Clearly there was something wrong with me, because I needed medicine to help me breathe.

We were also taught that there is no such thing as matter. Matter is just an illusion. What did that mean? That the sky didn't exist, the trees, my bed, our house, were all just illusions? Did that mean *I* didn't exist, that everything I was seeing, feeling, and thinking wasn't real?

Disease was what Mary Baker Eddy called "mortal error." When I was gasping for air, I had no time to think about the fact that my asthma was just an error. It took all my energy just to focus on the next breath. I was ashamed and blamed myself for not being smart enough to understand Mary Baker Eddy's teachings. I wanted to be one of those people who could say, "Guess what? I did it! I got it! I'm healed!"

Once, when I was 12, I went to a friend's house for an overnight. She used to ask me questions about Christian Science. She and her family seemed to make fun of it, and I was embarrassed. When it was time to get ready for bed and brush our teeth, she said, "But Eleanor, I thought there was no such thing as a tooth." *Right*. Why did I need to brush my teeth if they didn't exist? I didn't understand why it was OK to go to the dentist and the eye doctor, but not a medical doctor.

Although my mother was becoming increasingly committed to the ideas and writings of Mary Baker Eddy, she never denied medical help for the three of us, only for herself.

I didn't think of my asthma as a life-threatening disease; I just couldn't breathe some of the time. Like the time I went to a friend's birthday party and rode her new pony, even though I was severely allergic to most animals. I knew what would happen but wanted to be like everyone else. When it was my turn, I mounted the pony and rode one lap around the ring. Immediately I started gasping and wheezing. I couldn't breathe. My parents were called, and I was whisked away to the hospital for a shot of adrenaline. I wasn't frightened about not being able to breathe. All I could think about was what the other kids thought about me. I was ashamed.

During those elementary school years, I lived within the safety of a self-imposed cocoon. I silenced the voice inside that questioned my religious training. I followed the rules. Did my work. I kept the fear, the sadness, the confusion bottled up. I tried to pray but praying didn't help. I tried to get it. But in truth, nothing I was being taught in this new church made sense.

That cocoon began to unravel as I reached my teenage years. I was increasingly confused by the attention, or lack of it, from the boys on the Governor Dummer campus that I loved so much. When I was 13, I developed a crush on a boy named Sam. He had dark hair and blue eyes. He was athletic, sang bass in my father's glee club, and was captain of both the varsity football and baseball teams. We didn't spend much time together because faculty daughters didn't mix with students. But Sam and I were aware of each other's presence. At least, I was aware of his. I went to glee club rehearsals and to football and baseball practices and games. He knew I was there because often I caught him looking at me, and I didn't look away.

One afternoon, I was walking home from my piano lesson when I heard a voice behind me. "Hello, beautiful." It was Sam returning from football practice. I stopped when I heard his voice. My cheeks flushed, but I tried to look as though running into him didn't matter to me. The truth is, I spent most of my time trying to do just that. Now here we were, and I was blowing it. I looked down at his feet. I couldn't speak. Inscribed on his left sneaker was the name Louise. *Louise? Who is Louise?* I felt my stomach turn in knots. My ears were ringing, but somewhere in that din, I thought I heard the words "be my date." Every spring, the school held a dance where the boys could invite their girlfriends for the weekend. The boys slept on the gym floor while the girls slept in the dormitories. From the time I was little, I had watched girls arrive on campus for the weekend and dreamed of the day I might be one of them.

Was he actually asking me to be his date for that weekend? I wasn't sure I had heard correctly. Did Sam really like me? Did this mean I was his girlfriend? Was Louise already history? I don't remember how I answered. Maybe I decided to be cool and say that I would think about it. Regardless, for the next two days I fantasized about the way we would finally be together. We would be dancing, maybe holding hands, maybe even kissing. I imagined going with my mother to buy a dress. I dreamed about actually looking beautiful. I could already smell the gardenia Sam would give me.

But that dream was short-lived. Three days after he asked me to be his date, he changed his mind. He never said why. Instead, I watched him go to the dance with someone else. The gardenia would be hers.

Late one afternoon that following summer, my mother drove me to my friend Carol's house. I had been invited to a dance at an exclusive country club nearby. I didn't want to go, but my mother and Carol's mother thought this would be good for me.

Carol and I became friends because two of her brothers were students at Governor Dummer. One was a track star with an eye on the Olympics. Not surprisingly, he and my father had a strong connection. But I was hardly ever at their house.

I later learned that Carol's father did not approve of Carol's and my friendship. My father had created a public speaking business to supplement his income. Carol's father, a wealthy businessman, looked down on his endeavor because it wasn't listed in the Dun and Bradstreet report, whatever that was. Further, the country club membership was exclusive and required approval from a board that decided who was worthy of joining the club. My family would never have been approved. We were not on any social register and certainly not in the appropriate income bracket. I knew my family didn't belong there.

And yet, here I was, being driven up the long gravel driveway that crossed a small wooden bridge to Carol's house. It seemed like a mansion to me and was surrounded by acres of woods and streams. I glanced toward the backseat, where I'd placed the dress I'd borrowed from Jeannie: a light-blue, ankle-length gown with a net overlay. I could feel perspiration gather under my arms. How was I going to get through this? Most of the girls had dates. I would be alone at a dance where everyone knew everyone else. I knew I was not like them. I looked at my mother. I wanted to go home. But I said nothing.

I walked slowly to the front door, rang the doorbell, and waited. One of Carol's brothers opened it. No hello, no welcoming words, just an order: "Up there"—pointing to a winding staircase in the middle of a large entrance hall with high ceilings. An elegant sunken living room was off to the right. I obeyed the orders, climbed the stairs, and heard girls excitedly talking about their evening's dates. Two girls had spent the night and were taking turns soaking in a tub with rose-scented bath oil. Other girls were in front of mirrors applying makeup. I was not sure what I was supposed to be doing. I had no makeup to put on, so I stood around feeling invisible, watching and listening.

"Guess who Debbie invited to the dance?" said Penny.

"Who?" asked a chorus of curious girls.

"That cute guy from Exeter. Remember the one she had such a crush on?"

"Oh, yeah," said Dede. "I do. He is such a tweed!"

I wandered down the hall. There must have been ten bedrooms. One of the girls swept by me in a gorgeous full-length lavender gown with a wide pink sash at the waist. I found an empty room, changed into my dress, and looked in the mirror. I saw a plain 14-year-old with pasty skin, sweating nervously in a borrowed dress. I wanted a fairy godmother with a magic wand to turn me into someone like the others, someone who looked elegant and beautiful.

At the dance, I spent most of the evening on the sidelines, watching everyone waltz by me to the music of Lester Lanin. I tried to look nonchalant, with my chin up, lips together in a half smile, pretending that it didn't matter that no one noticed me. Every so often, a boy walked toward me, and I would think, *Maybe he's going to ask me to dance.* But he would pass right by as though I wasn't there. Carol and some of the girls saw me sitting alone.

"Eleanor, why do you look so sad?"

"Me? Oh, you're talking to me? I'm not sad, I just have those basset-hound eyes," I said, fake laughing as my brown eyes glazed over.

Chapter 3

"Time to go," my father called. He was using his everything-is-going-to-be-great! voice. I wondered if he had any idea what this day meant for me. My absence would not change his routine. He and my mother would be back home by dinnertime. I would not.

I was about to leave for Walnut Hill, a girls' boarding school ninety minutes away. I didn't want to go, but I knew I had no choice. There was no place for teenage girls on an all-boys campus. Day schools were not within commuting distance. That meant boarding school was the only option.

In those days, the school was too far away to come home from very often. We would be allowed four weekends a year, in addition to summer, Thanksgiving, Christmas, and spring vacations. When I was 11, I spent two months at a summer camp in the Berkshires. Throughout my stay, I pleaded with my parents to let me come home. That was out of the question. One of the expectations in my family was that you finish what you start. When my parents came to pick me up at the end of the season, they thought I was crying because I hated to leave. I was crying because I couldn't *wait* to leave.

As we pulled away from the familiar brick buildings and the bell tower, I stared out the window, holding back tears. I couldn't tell my parents what I was feeling. Jeannie had graduated from Walnut Hill in June. It would be so much easier if she was going to be with me, but she was on her way to college. There wasn't much conversation on the drive. I sat in the back seat looking out the window as each mile took me further and further from my home.

After my father parked in front of the brown stucco dorm that was to be my home for the school year, a student guide came over to welcome us. She helped us with registration and then accompanied us up a flight of mahogany stairs to my room, a narrow single room next to the infirmary. With the exception of the room across the hall, which was a single like mine, all the other rooms were doubles. My throat was tightening. I wanted to go back home to my own bedroom, with its white wallpaper and yellow daffodils. I wanted to go back to my little sister, who would grow up without me. I wanted to go back to 250 boys, not stay here with 150 girls.

My mother surveyed the room. A bureau and desk were shoved up against one wall, and the bed was against the opposite wall. "This isn't so bad," she said. "Maybe we should rearrange some of the furniture." We moved the desk in front of the window so that it looked out onto the residence where the kitchen help lived.

"Let's make the bed," my mother suggested. We worked together making hospital corners. We tucked a blanket in over the school-issued sheets and placed a colorful spread from home on top. As we placed my sweaters in a bureau drawer, she said, "If there is anything else you need, I can mail it to you." She slid the drawer shut. "And remember, it won't be long before we see you." This was the beginning of September, and the time until Parents' Day in October, when I would see them again, seemed like an eternity. I knew she was trying to make the best of the situation, but she didn't look at me as she spoke. I wondered what this was like for her, having to leave another daughter at boarding school.

I could hear my father's deep voice and big laugh resonating down the hall. He was already talking with other students and their parents. My father came back into what was now my room. "Guess what?" he announced. "I just met Debbie Cain. She lives in Connecticut and is right down the hall from you." He came over and stood next to me, looking pleased that he had launched my social life. "And you know Jackie Pallotta? His sister is here. She's going to come get you for lunch."

My father was already the most popular person on my floor. I knew he was trying to make things easier for me. He wanted me to see the sunny side of life. I just needed to put myself out there, he would often tell me. A few minutes later, my parents kissed and hugged me goodbye. My mother said she would write often.

I walked with them as far as the stairwell. I listened to their footsteps echo down the mahogany stairs, and from the large window on the landing, I watched them disappear into their car and drive away. I could hear the laughter and chatter down the hall. Maybe my father was right: Maybe I just needed to try. I walked back to my room and closed the door behind me.

Shortly after school started, two girls in my dorm decided to interview new students to determine who was cool enough to be part of their group. One by one, we were invited into their double room for questioning. Harriet asked things like, "Do you have a boyfriend?" Their criteria for acceptance were known only to them. They reminded me of the girls at the country club dance. I had a feeling having a boyfriend made a difference. I didn't have one, and I already knew I was different because, unlike these two and most of the other girls, I was on a full scholarship.

After the interview was over, I stood outside their closed door and heard them talking about me. "She has a big nose," said Harriet. No one was ever going to like me. I didn't have a boyfriend. And now it looked like I wasn't going to have any friends. I went back to my room and sat on the bed. After a few minutes I walked over to the mirror and examined my profile. Maybe I could change my nose. A pug nose would make a huge difference. Or a new personality. I knew one thing at that moment. I had to have friends. Otherwise, I would not survive this. It seemed like I was going to have to take a page from my father's playbook and put myself out there.

Since I couldn't participate in team sports due to my asthma, I found other activities. I made the glee club as the only sophomore. I joined the French Club, although I rarely attended a meeting. I was in the student government and secretary of the Polar Bear field hockey team, though I don't recall my responsibilities. I had been playing the violin since I was in the fourth grade, but I didn't want anyone to know that. It would not work with the persona I was trying to create.

Despite not making the cut with Harriet's clique, my efforts at putting myself out there were starting to pay off. I made some friends. I moved from my single room into a triple on the third floor with Mary Martha, Jackie Pallotta's sister, and Marsha, a girl from Martha's Vineyard. I was voted vice president of my dorm. Friends came home with me for the few weekends we were allowed off campus. The fact that I lived in a dormitory with forty boys was definitely a plus.

While things were improving socially, my schoolwork was slipping. I went from being on the honor roll to getting average grades because I got lost in my daydreams. I had a boy on the brain. The day before I left for school, Sam had come to our house and asked for my address. I probably shouldn't have agreed and let him get my hopes up again after the way he'd uninvited me to the dance, but I gave it to him anyway.

I lived for letters from him. A thin envelope meant a letter from my mother, which came every other day. A thick one meant a letter from Sam, which came about every three weeks. His letters kept me going. That spring, there was a dance at Governor Dummer with the Walnut Hill girls. When I stepped off the bus with the other girls, I saw him walking toward me. "Well, beautiful, are you coming?" He had never suggested in his letters that I would be his date for the evening.

It was magic. I was with the boy I loved. We danced together all night. The only person we allowed to cut in on us was my father. And then it was over. Just before we had to get on the bus to return to school, he asked if he could kiss me. That's all I had ever wanted. But I said no because I thought that might make him want me more. I boarded the bus and found a seat by myself. While the other girls giggled with excitement as they told each other about their dates and the evening, I was silent. I couldn't talk. No one could possibly understand my despair at having to leave this place that was so familiar to me, that was my home. I just wanted to be left alone. It was dark outside, but the darkness inside me was even deeper.

Sam didn't write to me after that. He graduated in the spring and went to college in Florida. I never saw him again.

Often I felt like crying but pretended to be happy. Walking to my dorm after study hall in the evening, I would peer in the windows of the houses across the street. The soft glow of lamps inside were warm and inviting, not like the harsh overhead lights in the dormitory rooms. I imagined families having dinner together, talking about their day. They could do whatever they wanted, go wherever they pleased. I couldn't. To me, it seemed like I was being held captive from my home and family. But what choice did I have?

My senior year, I was elected president of my dormitory. Granted, it was the smallest one on campus, but I didn't care. It was more of a popularity contest than a position of responsibility. I started drinking coffee, with lots of sugar. I laughed a lot, especially at myself. I learned how to inhale a cigarette, and I got drunk for the first time when our parents allowed four of us to go to Bermuda un-chaperoned. Mary Martha and I lived close enough that we saw each other occasionally during vacations and summers. One summer, we even made it through a debutante party together.

Church on Sundays was required. Most girls attended local churches in town, but another girl and I attended the Christian Science Church in Wellesley. It was much bigger than my church at home, though it was just as cold and spartan. The practice of Christian Science is based on the Christian Science Statement of Being, which says: *Spirit is God, and man is His image and likeness. Therefore, man is not material; he is spiritual.*

With the drone of the two readers in the background, I sat beside my friend, trying to push my fear of that cold nothingness away. Over and over again, I would say to myself, *Spirit is immortal Truth. Matter is mortal error*, still not understanding what that meant. No matter how hard I tried, nothing ever changed. I was ashamed of my asthma, ashamed of my feelings, and now I was ashamed of failing Christian Science.

Even though I gave the impression of fitting in, the popular, outgoing persona I had created was not me. But it had become me; I got lost in it to survive. Christian Science cemented the illusion that denial of dark emotions was the way to survive in the world. There was no one I trusted enough to say that I thought this was a lie, and I was miserable.

After graduation, I went to Wheelock College, a school that prepared young women to be teachers, but after a year, I knew I didn't want to be a teacher. I transferred to Boston University and majored in French, not because I had any passion for the language. It was simply a way to earn a degree. I graduated in 1963.

Not knowing who I was or what to do next, I allowed my father to arrange a meeting for me with a friend of his running for governor of Massachusetts. My job was to help with scheduling. After he lost the contest, I went to work for the Republican State Committee in Boston, which was championing Barry Goldwater in the presidential election. A right-wing extremist, Goldwater advocated cuts in social service programs and increases in military spending. He was willing to use nuclear weapons in the war in Vietnam. That kind of thinking scared me. Was he going to start another world war? I left that job, registered as a Democrat (much to the chagrin of my Republican father), and started working for an insurance company.

Occasionally, I attended Wednesday night testimonial services at the Christian Science Mother Church in Boston, looking for a way to fill the emptiness that clouded my thinking. I had no anchor. I found some comfort in the stories people told of their healings. There were no readings and no singing. People spoke when they felt moved to do so, and in between there was silence.

I would sit in the balcony, waiting to hear about something dramatic, something that defied reality. Maybe I could find it in these stories, but it never happened.

Chapter 4

Something smelled bad.

I was home for the weekend from Cambridge, where I was living with my friend Carol. As I walked from the breezeway into the kitchen, I knew something was wrong.

I said nothing to my mother or father about the odor and went upstairs to the room I shared with Perry when I was home. Passing by my mother's study, I noticed a letter on top of her desk. Although I felt I was invading her privacy, I walked into the room to take a closer look. It wasn't like her to leave letters exposed like that. The stationery was cream-colored with black typewritten script and a signature: *Mrs. Newcomb, Christian Science Practitioner*. When I read the signature, my mouth went dry. A practitioner is someone who prays for people who are sick. It was clear from the letter that my mother was in regular contact with her, and that she was ill. Earlier that year, I had noticed my mother occasionally touching her left breast, as though she was trying to feel something. I remembered wondering what that was about. I memorized the practitioner's name and telephone number, returned the letter to her desk, and quietly left the room. I knew I had seen something I wasn't supposed to see. The rank odor, even stronger upstairs, led me to the bathroom, where I found blood-tinged Telfa pads in the wastebasket.

On Sunday, I returned to Cambridge with Mrs. Newcomb's phone number in the pocket of my jeans, but I was nervous about calling. If she answered, I wasn't sure what I would say. Still, I slowly dialed the number. After the second ring, a woman picked up.

"Hello, this is Mrs. Newcomb."

I identified myself. "My name is Eleanor Sager."

"Oh yes, Mrs. Sager." My mother was clearly no stranger to her. I wasn't ready to hear more than I could take in, so I interrupted her.

"I'm not Mrs. Sager. I'm her daughter. I'm calling because I saw a note to her from you. Can you tell me if there is something wrong with my mother?"

There was a pause. "Well, dear, she is…" and then I heard only words. Their meaning didn't register, but I put the pieces together—the way my mother touched her breast, the bloody bandages.

I tried to gather enough composure to call my father, who had flown to New York earlier that day for business. I wasn't sure how he would react when I told him about the letter and the call I'd just made. But I had to know. There was a brief pause before he answered my question. "Your mother," he said, "has breast cancer." He actually said the words. Now it made sense. My father was a pipe smoker who often smoked after dinner. But now he smoked constantly when he was around her. It became clear that he was trying to hide the odor of untreated cancer. He told me that her brother, an internist at the New England Medical Center in Boston and on the faculty at Tufts Medical School, had offered to help her. She had turned down his offer.

I heard the strain in my father's voice when he said, "She does not want medical intervention."

I sat down on the couch, stunned, trying to take this in. She didn't want anyone to know. It seemed she wanted to keep this a secret from Jeannie, Perry, and me. I wasn't sure what to do.

According to the teachings of Christian Science, God's love is a healing power, stronger than any medicine. One way of demonstrating this is complete and total reliance on prayer. I kept hearing the words *Man is not material; he is spiritual* over and over again in my mind. My mother was treating her disease with only prayer.

She had made a choice, and that wasn't going to change. I could not imagine why she would refuse help from her own brother. Maybe she was afraid. Maybe her disease had progressed too far. Maybe she knew that and didn't want anyone interfering with what might be her only hope: her faith. And because I was afraid to ask her, I became an active participant in a terrible denial. The only person I shared this story with was Carol. Perry had given no clue that something was wrong at home, which made me suspect that she knew nothing.

Despite all the services I attended through my childhood and into college, I was not a Christian Scientist. And yet, at this moment, I dedicated myself to its teachings, trying to understand it. I started attending its church services again. I spent the next eight months reading Christian Science journals and attending weekly lessons that included passages of scripture and readings from *Science and Health with Key to the Scriptures* by Mary Baker Eddy. I met weekly with a Christian Science practitioner and tried to push my skepticism away.

I never asked my mother how she was feeling or if there was anything I could do for her. When I was home, I pretended not to notice the fetid odor or her weight loss. One morning, she had an Ace bandage around her ankle. My father told me he suspected it was broken. It never occurred to me that a broken ankle could mean that the cancer had spread to her bones. I tried to convince myself that if I ignored her symptoms, they might just go away.

That Thanksgiving, our family gathered at Jeannie's house in Connecticut. I noticed my mother could not stand over the stove for very long without resting. She took off her apron and went to the living room, where my father and Peter, Jeannie's husband, were watching football. My father kept his pipe lit. Perry entertained Jeannie's children. I got up to go see what I could do to help. Jeannie had gone outside to pick flowers for a centerpiece she was making. If she was aware of our mother's cancer, she said nothing.

"OK, what's going on with your mother?" Peter had followed me into the kitchen. He had noticed. I knew there was no way of hiding from him. I wanted to lie, but I couldn't. Truthfully, I felt a sense of relief that he suspected something. Peter was like the son my father never had. He had played football at Governor Dummer, was president of the glee club, and had been close to our family for years. He knew my mother's deep, unwavering commitment to Christian Science.

I told him.

"I'm taking El to the store. We need milk!" he called out. He was insistent about calling their family doctor, and we couldn't do that from the house. I was conflicted. I wanted to honor my mother's wishes—no medical intervention. This would be the second call to a stranger about her condition. Focusing on her symptoms was what I was trying *not* to do.

We drove five miles into the center of town and stopped at the first pay phone. Peter dialed the number. It seemed highly unlikely that a doctor would be willing to offer a medical opinion about someone he had never seen. But the doctor was a friend of theirs, and he agreed to speak with me. Peter handed me the receiver. I described the situation and told him what I had observed: the odor, the weakness, the bandages. He told me it sounded like her cancer was too advanced for medical treatment to be helpful. He paused and said, "From what you've told me, I suggest that her use of her faith is probably her best option."

How could I go back inside and pretend we had just run a simple errand when in fact we had confirmed a terrible truth? Peter did not want Jeannie to know, and I agreed not to tell her. Nor did I share this terrible secret with Perry. She was only 18, in her senior year of high school. Yet I knew how I would feel if they had information that would change all our lives and didn't share it with me. The weight of the denial grew heavier and heavier. I felt trapped, with no way out.

My mother's "illusion" kept worsening. She became so frail she was barely able to walk on her own. She had to take time off from teaching. Because medical help was out of the question, the best solution seemed to be the Christian Science Benevolent Association in Newton, Massachusetts, where Christian Scientists went for healing and rest. My mother disliked being away from home, yet it was she who suggested that spending time there might be helpful. Christian Science practitioners would be available to her every day, she said. She would get better and come home.

In January, my father took my mother's arm and led her slowly from the house to their car. Perry stood at the dining room window, and I stood at the living room window watching them make their way down the curved driveway to a place from which she would not return.

"How long have you known?" I asked Perry.

"Since June," she said. "How long have you known?" she asked.

"Since July," I replied.

We remained at the windows until the car was out of sight and then moved away without saying another word. The only clue to our feelings was the tears we tried, unsuccessfully, to hold back from one another. I was so busy trying to protect my mother, to save her life, even, that I had denied my sisters and myself the comfort we needed. I knew I couldn't undo the past seven months, but I made up my mind: I was going to move out of my apartment in Cambridge and come home to be with Perry.

I continued going to work. Perry continued going to school. I had no idea whether or not she was talking with anyone about what was happening in her life. I never asked. If I started to sound worried or morose, she would use her sidesplitting sense of humor to snap me out of it. During my senior year at Walnut Hill, I had been sent home with a severe case of the Asian flu; sick enough that the school did not want me back for a week. My first night home, Perry's imitation of me, lying feverish in bed, had me in such spasms of laughter that I could barely breathe. The next morning, my fever was gone and I was fine, with an unanticipated week's vacation in front of me.

The Benevolent Association was an elegant retreat center located on twenty-four acres of woodlands and gardens in Chestnut Hill. A tree-lined, winding driveway led to the 1919 asymmetrical brick building studded with dormers and turrets. Patients immersed themselves in the teachings of Mary Baker Eddy and were tended to by nurses trained in spiritual care as well as "comfort care." Comfort care included companionship when requested, clean sheets, daily meals, and loving presence; it did not include medications. The treatment for pain was always prayer, only prayer.

I visited my mother three or four times a week on my way home from work. On one early spring visit, she asked me to take her to the sunroom. This was a first. In the nearly two months she'd been there, she had shown no interest in being anywhere other than her room. She usually stayed in bed, listening to Christian Science lectures on tape or having someone read to her from Mary Baker Eddy's writings.

I felt a glimmer of hope. Maybe her desire to go out meant she was actually going to recover. As a nurse and I struggled to get her into a wheelchair, her nightgown slipped up, revealing part of her backside. She was skin and bones. More bones than skin. She was small to begin with, but now she couldn't have weighed more than 90 pounds. I had to look away.

I rolled her wheelchair to a large window in the sunroom that looked out over a garden waiting for spring cleaning. The snow was nearly gone, and the first signs of new life were visible. Purple and white crocuses peeked through the dead leaves. Birds were beginning to sing, and the tulips and daffodils were pushing up their green shoots. We didn't talk much. We were just a mother and daughter sitting in silence, watching spring emerge. And then she spoke.

"There are two things I want to say. I want to be sure you are sweeping the kitchen floor, and I want you to meet Peter Mercer." He was the new chaplain she had met at the end-of-year faculty party in June.

Although I didn't realize it at the time, this was clearly shorthand for *I'm dying. I don't have much time. Make sure things are in order at home and find someone to love—and not someone like the one you've been escaping to Vermont with on weekends.* I didn't know she knew about that. In spite of what I'd just seen, I told myself she was preparing me for her homecoming, not her death. I was in complete denial.

"Don't worry," I responded. "The floor will be swept when you come home, and maybe we can invite Peter over for dinner."

Three days after that visit, and nine months since I'd found the letter on her desk, I drove in a blizzard to see her. Slung over my arm was a bright orange dress I'd bought for a date I had that evening. I wanted to show it to her; I thought it might perk her up, perhaps even amuse her. Orange was definitely not my color. When I entered her room, still brushing the snow from my coat, the stench was pungent and overwhelming. Nothing could mask it, not even a pipe. I felt sick to my stomach. My mother was lying motionless on her back in bed. Her eyes were unfocused, open but not seeing me. She was searching to connect the sound of my voice with my location. When she tried to speak, only a jumble of nonsensical sound emerged. What I smelled was more than the odor of untreated breast cancer. It was the odor of death. My mother was in a room, dying, and I was alone. The dress fell from my arm onto the floor beside her. Rather than go to her, touch her, and offer comfort, I fled the room, looking for help. There was no one around. In my panic, as I ran down the hall, everything appeared barren. It looked like the paintings hanging on the wall in the hall had been removed. I couldn't see color or hear sounds. I needed someone here with me, someone to tell me what to do.

At that moment, my father was in the air, on a return flight from a trip to Bermuda. A trip that he and my mother had planned to take together, but she must have convinced him he should go without her. Jeannie was in Connecticut, and Perry was at a friend's house.

I didn't know if the storm would prevent my father's flight from arriving. I tried not to panic, although my heart was pounding. I needed a pay phone. My uncle. I needed to call him. I knew how much he loved her. But I didn't have his phone number, and I had only a few coins. I tried to understand the instructions on the front of the phone that was hanging on a wall next to the front entrance. I heard the clink of the dime as I placed my finger in the rotary dial to call information.

"May I help you?" asked the operator.

"I need the number for Dr. Joseph Rogers, in Milton." After she gave it to me, I had to keep repeating it over and over out loud, because I was afraid I would forget it. I didn't have enough money to call information again. I put the receiver back in the cradle to end the call, lifted it up once more, listened to the *clink-clink-clink* of the only coins I had left, and dialed his number. I hoped I had it right. Relief washed over me when I heard his voice.

"Uncle Joe, it's Eleanor. It's mom."

He was there in less than thirty minutes, despite the snow.

I stayed outside her room. I couldn't watch. I asked myself how things might be different if she had accepted his help several months ago. Worse, no one in our family had ever suggested she was dying. We had pretended it wasn't happening.

Twenty minutes later, my uncle came out of the room. He walked toward me and, in an unsteady voice, said he wasn't sure she would make it through the night. He had offered morphine to relieve what he could only imagine was significant pain. Even in her semi-comatose state, she had refused.

I watched my uncle leave, and I went home to be with Perry.

Perry needed her friends and her activities. She was now a senior in high school, and preparations were underway for the "Senior Frolics"—a tradition held each year by the graduating class. She and her friends were writing scripts, making costumes, creating set designs, choreographing dances, and selecting music. She wanted everything to be normal again. Normal meant going to school the way she always did. Only one friend and her friend's mother knew the truth.

During the years my father made weekly trips to New York for his public-speaking business, Perry and my mother had formed a special bond. They loved Monday nights, when it was just the two of them. They would cook their favorite meal, pasta with butter, and sit in the kitchen and talk. Perry would tell me how they'd laugh and laugh. She brought out a side of my mother I rarely saw, which was her dry sense of humor. The loss of my mother would devastate her. She wouldn't be there for Perry's graduation, or to help her get ready for college, or to see her off in the fall. But I couldn't think about that right now

My father's flight landed on schedule later that night. The next morning, Perry chose not to come with us to the Benevolent Association. When he and I arrived at my mother's room, the door was closed. My father paused. He took a deep breath and opened it. A nurse was with her. As soon as she saw us, she came out.

"There's been a change in your wife's condition," she said, looking at my father. I knew she was trying to be helpful, but the reality was that my mother's faith had not made her whole. This army of cancer cells was pure "matter," and they had invaded her 56-year-old body. My father had been away for a week. I wondered what was going through his mind as he stepped through the door. His wife of thirty-three years was not going to make it through the end of the day.

The nurse stayed outside the room while my father went in. I remained in a small sitting room, too afraid to watch her die. He wasn't in there long. "Oh shit," he said, his only words as he emerged from the room. I had never heard him swear before. He eased himself down onto a sofa and put his head in his hands. I wanted to comfort him, but I didn't know how. And so I sat and did nothing. The minutes ticked by as my mother lay on a bed, alone, with only a nurse by her side. I had never been with a dying person before, and I didn't want to be with one now.

On the table next to me were several editions of the *Christian Science Journal* and the *Christian Science Sentinel*, which included testimonials of healing. I picked one up. I had read many of these during the past few months. Christian Science claimed that complete submission to prayer, study, and correct thinking would lead to my mother's healing. It was a lie. I studied the lessons provided by the church each week. I read Mrs. Eddy's writings, which were incomprehensible to me. And still, my mother's body deteriorated, and the illness my family had been denying prevailed. The covenant my mother had forged with God had failed.

After a long hour, the nurse came into the waiting room. "It's over."

I put the journal down. I was done, finished. No more prayer. No need to keep reading Christian Science literature. No more church. This God that somehow was supposed to heal had no place in my life. My mother was dead. That's the only truth I needed.

Chapter 5

Three men in black suits rushed down the steps of the J.S. Waterman Funeral Home in Boston's Kenmore Square. Two of them parked cars, and the third handed us umbrellas. A cold rain was falling. My father, Perry, Jeannie, close family members, and I were directed to a dimly lit, windowless room set up with rows of chairs. The walls were a dreary gray-yellow color. As we took our seats in the front row, I noticed a few people sitting in back. Strangers to us. They must have been part of my mother's family, about whom we knew so little. I had no idea who had made the arrangements for this service or why it was being held here. At 11 a.m., a woman in a full-length dress appeared and took her place behind the lectern. She began reading from the Bible and *Science and Health*. She didn't speak about my mother; no one spoke about my mother. There was no reception. At the end of the service, we just went home.

Three weeks later, a large memorial service was held in the chapel at Governor Dummer. The sanctuary was filled with people who knew and loved her. Sun poured through the clear glass of the soaring, small-paned windows. There were flower arrangements on the steps of the chancel. And there was the new chaplain, Peter Mercer.

He had been asked by the headmaster to officiate. It was the first memorial service he had ever done.

My first thought when I saw him in his black robe standing behind the pulpit was: My mother was right. I should meet him. He was tall and handsome, with dark hair and green eyes. His voice and his words conveyed an authority and an authenticity that got my attention. I heard something about dreams, lilies, and dark clouds. It was more poetic than dogmatic. My heart beat a little faster.

The reception was a blur. I had only one thing in mind. I had to find this new minister. I needed to talk with him. I hated God. I hated church. A recent cover of *Time* magazine had declared, GOD IS DEAD. No one had to tell *me* that. I made up my mind to return to the chapel that same afternoon. I was carrying out my mother's final wishes—on my way to fall in love with the man who had just conducted her memorial service.

The daffodils in the garden in front of the headmaster's house were beginning to bloom. I drove past the building where the reception for my mother's service had just been held. The front doors of the chapel were unlocked. The sanctuary was cold and silent: empty pews, white walls, red carpet, and a few flowers left over from the service.

I made my way to the office in the rear and stood at the door, trying to gather the courage to knock. This new minister would wonder what I was doing there. I'd just turned to walk away when I heard him say "Hello?" I slowly opened the door to this office that doubled as a classroom. He was sitting behind his desk, smoking a pipe. My image of men who smoked pipes was that they were pensive, mysterious, and smart. I needed to spend time with him, maybe even the rest of my life.

Behind his desk, windows looked out onto a grove of pine trees that I knew well. I had played in those pines as a child, long before the chapel was even built. It was strange to be here in a place that was so familiar and at the same time so foreign.

Peter offered me a seat beside his desk. I didn't know how or where to begin. My mother was gone. "You didn't know my mother," I said, "but somehow I think she would have liked your service this morning."

My family and I had been in denial for so long we didn't know how to talk with each other about our feelings. I was done with Christian Science. But I had nothing to put in its place, and I had no idea what to do next.

Peter and I talked for over an hour.

As I was leaving, I asked if he would come have dinner at our house the following Sunday. He said yes.

Peter was smart. He cared about equal rights, compassion, and justice for everyone, not just a few. He didn't care about appearances and material wealth. He was a public-school boy who didn't know what a private school was until he needed a job and was offered a position at Governor Dummer. The elite world of secondary school life was completely foreign to him. He did not like dinner parties, cocktail parties, or cocktail-party talk. He turned down my invitations to show him what to wear to fit in. I knew what clothes to wear. These were the days of silver circle pins, kilts, knee socks, Shetland sweaters, and saddle shoes. I knew how to style my hair, which required sleeping on big fat rollers. I had learned what to do to be accepted. We were complete opposites, but everything about him appealed to me.

Every Friday night, he would escape campus life by traveling to a bar thirty minutes away in Portsmouth, New Hampshire. George's

Tavern sat on the corner of Ceres and Bow Streets and served beer, hot dogs, Campbell's soup, and pickled eggs. A big picture window at the end of the building overlooked the tugboats and the working docks. The regulars worked at the Portsmouth Naval Shipyard and included Conrad Ouellette, Joe Masqua, and Tom Marshall, who had their names carved on the first three barstools. One night, Peter walked in to find a label stuck to the fourth bar stool that read, "The Drunken Padre." When he invited me to join him one Friday night, I jumped at the chance.

We drove up Route 1 from Newburyport to Portsmouth, talking and listening to "Four Strong Winds" by The Brothers Four. When we arrived, he claimed his stool and I sat on an unmarked one next to him. "Hey, Pete, who you got there?" asked Tom, known as Tipperary Tom. And the introductions began. Peter was completely relaxed here. These were his people. No Harris Tweed jackets. No neckties and blue blazers. Just a few men in work clothes, winding down after a hard day of labor at the shipyard. I sat at the counter, drank beer, and ate hot dogs with Peter and the regulars. I stared at the pickled eggs, which looked like specimens soaked in formaldehyde. I was at home here because I was at home with Peter. That was the first of our regular Friday evening trips to Portsmouth.

One night, on our way back from George's, Peter told me that when he was a child, he had an incurable kidney disease. This was before penicillin was discovered. He never completed a full year of school until he was in the fourth grade.

Unable to play with other kids, he didn't learn the social skills that most children acquire in those early years. When he wasn't being tutored or doing schoolwork, he would take his pillows and blankets and create landscapes with his toy cowboys and horses. His friends were the people he listened to on the radio beside his bed: Fred B.

Cole talked and played music in the morning on WHDH; in the evening, *The Shadow* and *Sky King* kept Peter company.

One day, his temperature reached 105 degrees. The doctor told his parents he would not make it through the night and asked them to call when it was over. As his mother and grandmother took turns trying to sweat out the fever by wrapping him in hot towels, he said he could feel himself moving out of his body into an energy, which he described as completely embracing. He didn't want to come back. When morning came, he opened his eyes. The doctor was called.

Peter had had a brush with death, and it wasn't scary. Rather than feeling lost in a void, he had felt he was part of something he couldn't explain, and it was pleasant.

Peter had a spiritual anchor. Not me. Maybe he could help me find one. Being around him made me feel grounded.

Chapter 6

I dropped my bag of groceries on the counter and walked into the living room to say hello to my father. It was June, three months after my mother's death. Sitting close to him was an attractive woman in her late forties with short brown hair and a trim figure. She had a cigarette in one hand, and her other hand was in my father's. I didn't know he had company. "Oh, hi," I said, trying to sound casual. He introduced me and said that Frieda had lost her husband in March. So this was the woman he had told us he'd been introduced to a few weeks earlier. My mother had never smoked, and I never remember my father holding hands with her. My stomach twisted in knots.

In August, they announced they were planning to be married in October. Frieda, fourteen years younger than my father, had two children. One was a junior in high school, one a sophomore in college.

Jeannie was a young mother with four children. Perry was busy with a summer job and friends. The insurance company I was working for in Boston had invited me to be part of a program training new agents. Not only was I not qualified, but I couldn't imagine finding fulfillment in the world of insurance. I was afraid to turn down the offer, though, because it was all I had. My mother was dead. My father was remarrying. We were all moving in different directions.

That summer, I went to visit Peter on Star Island, a Unitarian Universalist/United Church of Christ conference center located on the Isles of Shoals off the coast of New Hampshire. Star Island was central to Peter's life—he'd worked there for the past ten summers— and he wanted to share it with me. Having seen how quickly I had become comfortable around his friends at George's, he assumed I'd fit right in.

He met me at the dock, and we walked up the hill to the massive Victorian hotel overlooking the harbor. The wraparound porch was lined with rockers, and the spacious lobby harked back to the grand hotel era of the turn of the last century, albeit with much of the grandeur worn away by time and traffic. Peter went off to work, and I climbed the creaky stairs to the third floor and found the room I was assigned. For a moment, I had a flash of arriving at boarding school. How tempting it would be to just hole up here until Peter could show me around, but then I heard my father's voice: *Put yourself out there.*

That didn't prove to be so easy. The staff was busy with their jobs. Peter was busy with his. The conferees were involved with lectures, meetings, and planned activities. I took walks out to the rocky back shore of the island, visited the marine biology lab, spent time in the bookstore, and waited for someone to acknowledge my existence. But it didn't happen. I tried to look like I belonged somewhere, but the truth was, I was an outsider. Other than a woman who worked behind the front desk, no one spoke to me. It became clear that I was infiltrating a tight network of people devoted to Peter. I was not part of this club.

After two days, I packed my bags and told Peter I was leaving. We walked down to the pier together, perhaps feeling a little awkward that this hadn't turned out as either of us had hoped or planned. Our goodbye was brief as I got on the boat back to the mainland.

There is a Star Island tradition: When the boat pulls away, people on the pier shout, "You will come back! You will come back!" and those leaving respond, "We will come back! We will come back!" It's based on a legend about one of Blackbeard's wives, whom he had abandoned on the Shoals. The story goes that Shoalers can see a shadowy figure on the rocks, mournfully calling, *He will come back. He will come back.* At that moment, I kind of knew how she felt.

As I watched the distance between the boat and the island increase, I muttered to myself, "I will never be back." But what was I going home to? A job I didn't want. No Peter. God was dead. My family, as usual, wasn't talking about the events of the past few months. I was afraid of spending the rest of my life alone.

One week later, I was recovering from a tonsillectomy. I took a pill to help with pain that relaxed me enough to find the courage to call the insurance company and decline their offer. Now what was I going to do? Find a job as a teacher or a secretary? Never. I had to find something that excited me.

So I went on a search. After sending out several résumés, I was hired by Trans World Airlines—or TWA, as it was better known—as a ground hostess at Logan International Airport. I listened to peoples' stories as they boarded planes for Europe, and I assisted non-English-speaking people on incoming flights. I sat with the Mother Superior who tossed down a bourbon just before her flight to France. I served as a confidante to a German Olympian. I was the target of an Italian actress who was angry that her delayed flight would affect her filming schedule. When I wasn't working, I kept myself busy trying to find a way out of my deepening darkness. If I let myself fully go there, I wasn't sure how I would climb out.

And then one evening after work, I heard a car coming up the driveway. I went to the window and saw Peter's green Mustang. I had thought we were done. I considered pretending I wasn't home, and then the doorbell rang. I was too scared to let him back into my life, and even more scared to let him walk away. My heart skipped a few beats. I opened the door.

We began spending most of our free time together.

At the same time, Perry was preparing to attend Lindenwood College in St. Charles, Missouri. I had been so obsessed with my own despair after our mother's death, that I did little to help my younger sister through the end of high school. I have no idea how she was able to apply and get into college while her world was falling apart. Her closest childhood friend later told me she thought Perry felt that my mother had chosen Christian Science over her, and she was angry. She was probably angry at all of us. But instead of talking about it, she managed on her own. The message in my family was move on— and so she did.

Perry and I climbed into the backseat of my father's Chrysler convertible to take her to Logan Airport. Frieda was in the front seat beside my father—where our mother should have been. She had a package of Kent cigarettes in her bag and offered me one. I lit it; it helped take the edge off the anxiety building over being separated from Perry. I didn't want her to leave. Jeannie and I had tried to convince our father that this wasn't the time for Perry to go out into the world by herself. My mother hadn't been gone six months, and my father and Frieda's wedding would be in less than two months. This all felt so wrong.

Perry was wearing a bright tie-dyed shirt with slim jeans that showed off her figure. She had recently ruined the piercings in her ears by wearing large earrings with glass balls. But that didn't deter her. She just started wearing even larger clip-ons. Her selection for this day was a pair of purple, shimmery, four-inch-long hoops. Protruding from her hip was her prized shoulder bag, handmade from a gourd. She looked like she had a tumor.

As we approached the airport, Perry and I became quieter and quieter. When it was time to say goodbye, I stood at the window watching her walk across the tarmac. Once again, we were at different windows not able to see each other's tears. Only this time it was Perry who was leaving. As the plane taxied down the runway, everything in me was screaming, *Stop that plane! Don't take our Precie away!* But I didn't say a word.

After a month, it was clear that being far away was the wrong move. She wanted to come home, and Jeannie and I wanted her with us. For weeks, we pleaded with my father to get her out of there, but he was firm in his belief about finishing what you start. Jeannie and I approached Frieda, because we knew he would do anything she asked. She agreed with us that Perry should come home. And her daughter, a junior in high school, could use a sister.

After a month, Perry was back.

Frieda wore a cream-colored, tea-length dress she had made for their wedding. My father bought a Hickey Freeman suit. My sisters and I told each other we were relieved to see our father happy again, but everything had happened so fast. I never questioned my father's love for us, but his life was now focused in another direction. He had a new family.

My father and Frieda moved into her house while they looked for a new place to live. Perry had plans to go to Lasalle Junior College in Boston. Jeannie moved back to Massachusetts with her husband and their three children, soon to be four. Her husband's job with a marine hardware company brought them to Boston.

Like me, Jeannie had wanted to support our mother's way of dealing with her illness. Like me, she read, prayed, and worked on trying to visualize our mother as she was on the inside—whole, not ill. Unlike me, however, she began attending the church where my mother had held membership. I understood. We were all looking for answers in our own ways.

Three months later, I stood with Perry and Jeannie at the window of my childhood friend Nan's apartment, watching guests arrive.

"Look, there are George and Kay and their boys."

"Oh, and there's Kate and John."

Our chatter helped take the edge off my nerves. I turned around to see my father standing behind us smiling. I knew what that meant, but I needed a moment to collect myself. So, with shaking fingers, I straightened his tie, even though it was perfectly knotted. When I was done, I looked up into his eyes.

"Time to go," he softly said. I took a deep breath, slid my arm through his, and we made our way next door to the chapel where he and Frieda had walked down the aisle just two months earlier. Only this time, it was my turn. I was about to marry Peter Mercer.

This was not the fairytale wedding I had imagined since childhood. Everything felt thrown together. Carol's mother altered her elder daughter's wedding dress to fit me. She repaired my mother's long antique veil, delicately sewing lace in the sheer fabric. She ordered the flowers and gave me a bridal shower. She addressed invitations with me, bought Peter and me everyday dishes, and planned the reception. She did everything she could to help Peter and me get started in our life together, all the things she knew my mother would have done. I was so lucky to have her, because otherwise I didn't have a clue.

As I waited in the back of the church, ready to process, Frieda was escorted down the aisle to the seat where my mother should have sat. Her presence there made us look like a family. We were not. We barely knew each other.

Nine months after her death, my mother had been erased, just like that.

Chapter 7

Peter and I settled in to getting to know each other. I moved into his tiny, third-floor apartment in the same dormitory where I had spent the first seven years of my life. It had a living room and a bedroom with a hotplate and a refrigerator. If we wanted to use the hotplate, we had to call the couple in the apartment below us and ask them to unplug their refrigerator.

Many people assumed this rushed marriage meant a baby must be on the way. But it wasn't like that. Even though we'd only been seeing each other for six months, we knew we belonged together. We felt if we waited to get married, it wouldn't happen.

The following year, we moved to Newton, Massachusetts, so that Peter could finish his last year of seminary at Andover Newton Theological School. When we returned to Governor Dummer, the school offered us a small 1700s house with two bedrooms, a renovated kitchen, a dining room with a big fireplace, and a living room. A real home.

Erik was born that spring, and Tim followed two and a half years later. I was alone with the children most of the time. Peter was teaching and coaching. He was required to eat meals in the dining room and do dormitory duty several nights a week. My days were filled with nap times, bottles, laundry, cleaning, and cooking while Erik and Tim played. Their favorite toys were the contents of the kitchen cupboards, which they never got tired of spreading all over the floor. We read books, took walks, watched *Sesame Street* and *Mister Rogers*. Sometimes we got together with my friend Nan who had children the same age.

Before Erik arrived, I had never even changed a diaper. Parenting was all new to me. I depended on experts like Dr. Spock and Haim Ginot to guide me. I needed someone to reassure me that what I was doing wouldn't damage my children for life. Jeannie and I talked on the phone almost every day. She was a wonderful mother and offered me lots of support, but she was busy with four young children, which meant I rarely saw her. Perry had finished college and had gone to St. Croix with a friend for a few months. Frieda was not interested in children and was settling into a new life with my father. I had to figure out how to be a parent on my own.

One day, I was trying to carry Tim upstairs for his afternoon nap. I couldn't get beyond the first two steps because I couldn't breathe. For days, I had been using an over-the-counter inhaler every half hour to survive. I never told Peter that I was in trouble, because I didn't even know I was. I thought the inhaler was helping me. But when it became clear that I didn't have enough breath to take care of my children, I got scared. If I was going to get through this episode, I had to confess that I needed help. I called my uncle, who made arrangements for me to see a doctor at the New England Medical Center.

The next day, Peter drove me to Boston. "You actually walked in here on your own?" the doctor said in disbelief when he saw me. He helped me get up on the examining table and, without saying a word, gave me an injection. I didn't have the breath or the time to ask him what he was putting in my arm. Later in the day, when it was safe for me to go home, I knew I would have to be on some kind of medication permanently. I never did ask him about the injection. I was just grateful that it worked, and that I would be able to pick Tim up again. That was all that mattered.

Peter was anxious to get out of Governor Dummer and into church ministry. Ten months after Tim was born, he accepted a position at a small church in Maine. It had a beautiful colonial parsonage with a view of Casco Bay. The fledgling congregation began to grow with Peter's leadership, going from nearly closing its doors to over 100 members in two years.

Because the church didn't pay enough to cover our basic expenses, Peter was forced to supplement our income by bartending on Saturday nights at a local pub. This meant church for some of the faithful began the night before, with something a little stronger than communion wine in their cups. It was hard watching him come home at two a.m. and then have to be at the church by eight the next morning.

I considered going back to school for a degree in psychology, but I wanted more than a study of human development and behavior. I was still searching for a spiritual anchor. Instead, I served on committees at the church. Betty Friedan had just published *The Feminine Mystique*, and the women's movement was growing. I was invited to join a women's consciousness-raising group. All of us were considering our next steps, as our children reached school age; some already had part-time jobs. The conversations revolved around how to achieve a balance between work and home, and how to make our voices heard in a society dominated by men.

I joined the Junior League and chose working with incarcerated teens as my volunteer service. Once, a 12-year-old boy told me he had been accused of stealing his mother's diamond ring. I listened to him tell ahis story and believed him. The staff called me naïve, said this was a manipulative kid just trying to win me over. That was probably true. But I felt my role had nothing to do with judging his innocence or guilt, his truth-telling or his lies. It had everything to do with listening to his version of what happened. Something began to stir in me. I was starting to find a direction to guide me: It's peoples' stories that matter.

Still, I was struggling when by all measures I should have been thriving. Peter and I had two healthy children and a gorgeous place to live. My sisters and my father were less than two hours away. I was now managing my asthma with medication. I had a solid, safe life.

Except that my inner life was beginning to unravel. I became terrified of anything that might take me from my husband and sons or take them from me. Flying was out of the question. I kept the depth of my shame about my fears a secret from everyone, including Peter. The confident persona I presented to the world was so convincing, no one had any idea that I was falling apart inside.

When my father called, suggesting I go with him and his new family while he taught a public speaking course in Bermuda, I panicked. He felt a change in air would help my asthma, but I was too afraid to get on a plane. I came up with every excuse I could think of: I don't have anything to wear. We would need someone to come in and help Peter with the children, and we can't afford that. But my father offered to cover all expenses.

I had to go. I couldn't invent any more reasons for needing to stay home. For a week, I was consumed with thoughts of crashing, of our children being abandoned by me. No one could ever love them the way I did. How could I get out of this? How could I say no to my father, who adored me, worried about me, wanted me to be healthy, and offered me an all-expense-paid vacation in Bermuda? Everyone would know I was crazy, and I was beginning to think I was, too.

One week later, I met my father, Frieda, her mother, her daughter, and two of their friends Logan Airport. I could see my father at the ticket counter, talking with the agent. He knew I was afraid to get on a plane. Because the flight he and the others were on was oversold, he had made a reservation for me on a later flight and intended to take that seat. I would take his on the earlier flight.

I could see there was a problem. He walked back to me and told me that FAA regulations wouldn't allow the switch. I had to take the later flight. We looked at each other, stunned and helpless. "I can't do it, Dad. I am so ashamed, but I can't get on that plane alone."

There was no time for discussion. The flight had been announced, and he had to go. I stood watching him move up the escalator, looking back at me. My heart broke as I saw tears in his eyes.

As they disappeared, I collapsed in a chair and dropped my head in my hands. How was I ever going to tell Peter and the rest of my family and friends that I was coming home? I was so ashamed.

Suddenly, the ticket agent ran out from behind the counter and grabbed my hand. "Come with me!" I had no time to think or ask what was going on. We tore up the escalator, down the bridge toward the plane, just as it was beginning to pull away. He grabbed an intercom that gave him access to the pilot and commanded, "Stop that plane!" I stood there stunned as it rolled back in. The door opened. "She's sitting with you," he yelled over the sound of jet engines to the bewildered flight attendant. "Don't ask questions." He signaled to my father in coach that I was on the plane. With no time to protest or panic, I buckled my seat belt, closed my eyes, and held on. After the plane was in the air, I was served a first-class champagne breakfast. I waved back to my father and his family, as they were chewing on their economy-class biscuits.

Chapter 8

I stood on the front lawn of the parsonage, watching three men take everything from our home of the past four years. Peter had accepted a call to a larger church, and we were moving two hours north to Bangor. The moving van was parked in the driveway where Erik loved to ride his Big Wheel and where Tim used his toy tools to help the carpenters fix shingles on the barn.

It had been a hectic morning. But now the reality of what was happening suddenly caught up with me: We were going to have no home for several hours. The panic of floating alone in space gripped me. It was so hot. I felt dizzy. I sat down on the ground and passed out. When I came to, a terrible anxiety began to take hold of me. A friend brought me to her house while the movers finished their job. I didn't talk with her, or anyone else, about my fear of being untethered and isolated. It was too humiliating.

Things only got worse with the move. Perry, Jeannie, and I talked often, but they seemed so far away. Perry was now married with two children and living in Connecticut.

My fear continued to grow. I avoided anything that involved risk. I was obsessed with the wellbeing of my family. I was terrified that one of them might get sick and not tell me. Peter's physicals always showed too much protein in his urine. I worried about his kidneys. Anytime either of the children had a symptom, no matter how small, I took them to the doctor. What if I didn't do everything I could to keep them from getting sick and dying? Or me, their mother? I became hypochondriacal. I was sure I was going to get breast cancer. My world was closing in. I was too afraid to go to the grocery store. I didn't travel to unknown places. If I took a walk, I couldn't go more than two blocks before I felt as though I was going to pass out. There were days I would sit on the edge of the couch afraid to go to the store for a carton of milk. If I went to the movies or found myself in large groups, I searched out the exits and always had to have an aisle seat. I had become a prisoner in my own world, which was growing smaller and smaller.

The summer after we moved to Bangor, we went to visit my father and Frieda, who had returned to their home in Boxford, Massachusetts, from their winter house in Florida. Peter and the boys were outside by the swimming pool. Frieda was on an errand with her daughter, and I was alone in the kitchen, folding laundry. It was midafternoon, and the glass doors leading to a flagstone patio were open. A breeze carrying the sound of the boys squealing and jumping off the diving board came through the doors. I had one eye on the children and one eye on the laundry. As I was folding the last sheet, I could smell my father's cherry pipe tobacco coming closer. I turned around to see him walking into the kitchen, his pipe between his teeth.

He stood against the butcher block. We chatted about his work. After a few minutes, I gathered the courage to change the topic. This was the perfect time to talk with him alone.

"Dad, are you happy?"

His eyes filled with tears. "I've never been happier in my life." This felt like a punch in the gut. What did that mean about his relationship with our mother?

He continued, "Your mother was a wonderful woman, but our backgrounds were different. I always felt she was better than me." He paused and then said, "When she was eighteen, she had a nervous breakdown." He never changed his expression.

A nervous breakdown? I asked him for details, for more information, but he had none. He only knew the facts, not the causes or the treatment, if there had been any. He gave me a hug and asked if I was OK. When I assured him I was fine, he walked back to his study to make some phone calls, leaving me to take all this in on my own.

In the following months, as I continued trying to sort things out, it began to make sense. I gathered that any talk about depression or sadness was not tolerated in my mother's family. Maybe that led to her interest in Christian Science while she was a student at Mt. Holyoke. Perhaps she was trying to find her way out of her own prison.

One day when I was leafing through her papers, looking for answers to what might have caused a "breakdown," I came across several pieces of poetry that were clearly hers. Some of the poems were typewritten on lined notebook paper, which had discolored with age. One was handwritten on desk notes with my father's name at the top, *Arthur W. Sager*. She had crossed out words and made changes in ink. The writing was so formal, it was as though a stranger had written these pages.

One of the poems revealed the thoughts of a woman who struggled with a difficult past. It described being sad and "forlorn." Another poem suggested a mystical experience. On an August night, she wrote that a beam of light coming from "distant skies" had passed deep inside her. She closed her eyes, "opening her soul" to something beyond her understanding. The poem ended with a plea to God, asking that He let that light pass through her on days when her vision became clouded.

As I studied her words, I caught a glimpse into my mother's secret, inner life. I discovered a woman I never knew but wished I had: a woman who tried to make sense of injustice and inequality in the world, as I do; a woman whose struggles led her to a faith so deep that she was willing to test it, even to her death; a woman with whom I could, perhaps, have spoken about feeling sad and afraid of being alone. Searching for clues to her, I realized they had been there all along. I just wasn't paying attention. Or I just wasn't ready to see the message hidden behind the words.

My anxiety got to the point where I never traveled anywhere without Peter. The thought of being caught in traffic terrified me. I always had an excuse for what I couldn't do or where I couldn't go. My friends and family believed me. When Perry was in the hospital for three months with a broken pelvis, I said I couldn't drive the five hours to visit her because my part-time job, working with teenage girls in a group home, left me no time. I had stooped that low with my excuses and lies.

One evening, I was standing at the kitchen sink, washing the dishes and watching the first snow of the season. Winters in Bangor could be long and bleak, and this one was shaping up to be no exception. Peter was at a conference in Pennsylvania, and I was alone with the children. Erik and Tim were playing in the family room. I glanced at the small black-and-white TV on the kitchen counter. The tail end of a program grabbed my attention. I stopped, took my hands out of the dishwater, and stared as a woman staggered down the aisles of a store, sending elegant vases and goblets crashing to the floor.

Oh my God, that's me! In that moment, I saw myself on that screen, and knew exactly what she was experiencing. I noticed a word in the credits: *agoraphobia.* I rushed to the Merriam-Webster dictionary and looked it up: "Agoraphobia is a type of anxiety disorder in which you fear and avoid places or situations that might cause you to panic and make you feel trapped, helpless, or embarrassed." I may not have known the word, but it had suddenly become my world.

I needed help. I picked up the phone and called the one person I knew I could trust, the associate minister in Peter's church. I was desperate, and she was nearby. "I'm in trouble, Ansley." In ten minutes, she was at our house. She stayed until Erik and Tim were in bed and I had calmed down. Peter cut his meetings short and came home the next day. The following morning, Ansley arrived with an article from the *New York Times* on agoraphobia. After years of hiding, I suddenly had a name for what was wrong with me. I made up my mind, then and there, that I was not going to live my life this way. It was time to do something.

I began to see a behavioral therapist. That didn't help. I wanted an anchor like the one Peter had. Bangor Theological Seminary was a few blocks from our house. I enrolled. Maybe I'd find some answers there. I was willing to try anything.

Sitting in a class on the New Testament one day, unable to focus, my mind began to wander to a paper I was writing about the similarities and differences in the four gospels. I looked over at the clock. It was noon. *Tim! Oh no!* He was in nursery school, and I had forgotten he was there. I was so absorbed in wondering what I was doing in this class that I completely forgot about the time. I, who was terrified of abandonment, had just abandoned my own child. I had to get out of there—the class as well as Bangor.

We had been in Bangor for only three years, and Peter wasn't ready to leave. He would be making a big professional sacrifice to leave the church so soon, but he was committed to my getting better. He accepted a call to a church in Lowell, Massachusetts.

We stayed only two years in Lowell. The church had not been open with him about the extent of its dysfunction, and the principal of the school where we sent our children was interested in order, not education. The only salvation was that we were closer to our families, and I was able to complete a year of Clinical Pastoral Education, training for hospital or hospice chaplaincy, a requirement for a Master of Divinity. For the first part of the year, I was assigned to a psychiatric ward in a local hospital. After each visit, we were required to write a "verbatim," a detailed description of the setting, the smells, the sounds, as well as the dialogue, or lack of it, with the patient.

One day, I was chosen to be the target of our twice-weekly supervision session. Good, I thought to myself, because I'd just written a really solid verbatim. I presented my visit with a patient who was an amputee with stumps that he wiggled in front of me as soon as I got near him. The priest let me go on for a while, and then he interrupted me.

"What it was like for you when the patient began to wiggle his stumps?"

"Oh, it was fine," I said. "I didn't even really notice."

He shot me a look. "Wait just a minute. Stop right there. You're telling me you didn't notice that he was missing his legs?" I could feel my face getting red. He continued to press until I had to admit that I found it disgusting. I was furious with him for seeing under my nice-girl cover. Who was he to question me? What did he know about anything? He was too young to do what he was doing. He didn't even have a family. I rushed out of class when it was over.

This young priest had broken through and exposed my façade of pretending not to notice a man with no legs, just the way I pretended not to notice my mother's broken ankle, or the terrible smell of un-treated cancer, or that I was afraid of illness, dying, losing my family. He did exactly what he was supposed to do, and I hated him for it.

Chapter 9

Two years later, Peter and I accepted positions at Suffield Academy in Connecticut. Peter would serve as the chaplain, with additional teaching and coaching duties. My title was Director of Counseling. I would oversee an advisor–advisee program, as well as a dormitory of twenty junior and senior girls. I had no idea what I was signing on for. The extent of my qualifications was a course in pastoral counseling, plus one year of clinical pastoral education. Still, I told myself, I can do this. I've lived most of my life in dormitories. I know the drill. And, if the school was willing to take a chance on me, I was ready to try anything. Furthermore, we were out of Bangor, and Suffield offered a good education for our children.

My office, located in the basement of the classroom building, served as a drop-in center for students who wanted to talk. I found I was able to connect with those who were homesick, anxious, or feeling pressure to fit in and perform academically or athletically. I knew what it was like to feel out of place, and I knew the importance of just having someone with whom to share those feelings. So I listened. I handed out tissues. I didn't offer a lot of solutions, but I tried to create a safe environment where they could openly discuss things that were difficult to talk about. I wish I'd had a place like that when I was a teenager.

One year when spring vacation rolled around, my father invited me to be part of his teaching team for a course he was offering at a bank in New York City. He had recently published a book called *Speak Your Way to Success* and was offering courses to business executives, both nationally and internationally. From time to time, he suggested I might want to be more involved in this work. But I knew myself well enough to know that I was more interested in listening to people's stories than I was in helping men, primarily white men, write speeches designed for success in business.

Still, I accepted his offer. I knew that a trip into the city would mean negotiating a train transfer in New Haven and hailing a cab on my own to get to the hotel. That was a gamble for me and my agoraphobia, but I had to keep saying yes to these opportunities if I was ever going to be free.

Peter dropped me off at the Windsor Locks train station. The transfer went smoothly in spite of my anxiety. I managed to change trains just like everyone around me. Three hours later, we arrived at Penn Station. I'd made it. I walked up to the street level, where a light snow was falling, and found a long line of commuters waiting for cabs. Traffic jams and lines were triggers for me. I began to panic, but I took my place with the others. *You are not going to pass out,* I told myself over and over again. *You'll be in a cab soon.* I focused on my breathing and looked around to see if there was anyone who might help me if I got into trouble. I reminded myself: You are not alone in the city. All you need to do is make it to the hotel.

When I eventually stepped out of the cab and into the lobby, it felt like a giant leap.

Even though I was making headway with my agoraphobia, I still struggled. I continued making excuses for not being able to travel or fly. It took all my energy to drive to Boston two days a week for classes I was taking at Andover Newton Theological School. I concealed my constant worry about my own and my family's health. When I discovered a thickness in my right breast, I convinced myself I had breast cancer. A doctor in Connecticut suggested the mass or even the breast might need to be removed. I became obsessed, constantly checking the area, just as my mother had done. After a second opinion from a doctor in Boston, and a biopsy, the thickness turned out to be normal breast tissue.

I even managed to deny my own fear to myself. Fear did not apply to me; fear was always someone else's problem. However, my dreams suggested otherwise. Too often, I dreamed I was trapped in prisons or in basements, with no way out. And whenever I went out in public, I still made sure I knew where the exits were.

No matter how hard Peter and I tried to make our years in another private school work, he was still a public-school boy in an elite world. After eight years, he knew he had to make a change. He wanted to be back in a church, and after the sacrifices he'd made for me in leaving Bangor, I was prepared to support whatever he needed to do next. He accepted a call to parish ministry in Easthampton, Massachusetts. I remained at Suffield so Tim could finish his senior year. Easthampton was close enough that I could visit Peter on the weekends. With Peter's leaving, I was invited to assume the role of the school's chaplain.

My asthma seemed to be under control, but the eczema I'd had since childhood had returned with a vengeance. It now covered every part of my body except my face. I wore turtleneck jerseys with long sleeves, and skirts with tights underneath. I thought I was fooling everyone, but I couldn't hide the scratching to relieve the incessant itch.

At the end of the year, the senior class held an event in which they parodied the Suffield faculty. When they got to me the students rolled up their sleeves and pretended to scratch and scratch, I laughed along with them, but I was embarrassed. I wasn't aware of my behavior because it was so much a part of my life. Only kids would have the courage to call it out.

I made an appointment with a well-known Boston dermatologist. When I arrived in his office, he rattled off the names of all the celebrities he had treated. I felt privileged he'd found time in his busy schedule to see me. If he could help all the people he'd told me about, he could certainly help me. After a brief examination, he recommended the following formula: Go home and soak in a tub three times a day, apply cortisone ointment, wrap yourself in Saran Wrap for an hour or two, remove the wrap, and polish the treatment off with Hydrolatum, a hard-to-find over-the-counter cream. His Hollywood patients probably had time to relax in Saran Wrap, but I did not. I was working, writing papers, taking exams, cooking, cleaning, trying to hold things together. I tried it for a week. I did not improve.

Because I needed one more Old Testament credit to graduate, I signed up for a course on the Book of Job. Here was a story about a man who lost everything, including his entire family. His friends tried to help him by asking what he had done. Catastrophes like this don't just happen without a reason, they said. But Job was a good man of deep faith. He told them he had done nothing wrong. He'd never even looked at another woman. He was *that* good. Finally, when he was stripped of everything except the sackcloth he was wearing and covered with sores, he cried out from the ash heap on which he sat, "Why God? Why me?"

God answered his plea out of a whirlwind. "Gird up your loins like a man. I will question you, and you shall declare to me." God then peppered Job with four chapters of questions, such as, "Where were you when I laid the foundations of the earth? Tell me if you have understanding." "Where is the way to the dwelling place of the light, and where is the place of darkness?" "Can you lift up your voice to the clouds, so that a flood of waters may cover you?"

Job listened until, exhausted, he conceded that if there were answers they were beyond his understanding.

As I slowly closed the book, the message began to sink in. It was so still and quiet in my office, I could hear myself breathing. Suddenly, I pushed back in my chair and laughed. Of course! I got it. In one instant, my search for spiritual authenticity had an answer, and guess what? The answer was that there isn't one. It's the search that matters.

I thought back on all the years I'd spent reading, studying, working with practitioners, attending services, taking classes, accepting all the doctrines I'd been fed—trying to understand something that wasn't there. Job's story gave me the freedom to move forward. My true spiritual journey had begun.

Around this time, I discovered the Gospel of Thomas, one of the gnostic gospels that were excluded from the New Testament when it was formed in 325 AD. The gnostic gospels, considered heretical in many churches, were focused on inner spiritual reality, rather than dogma. In Thomas, I read: "Those who seek should not stop seeking until they find. When they find, they will be disturbed." That's what had been missing for me all these years. It was permissible—and even necessary—to be disturbed. I didn't have to keep my disgust, my fear, my agoraphobia a secret. It took too much energy to pretend that everything was fine when it wasn't. It was time to expose those dark places to the light.

I began to ask myself what I was doing with my life. I'd spent four years working on a Master of Divinity, sacrificing time I could have spent with our children. How many times had they asked me to play Monopoly or Clue with them, and how many times had I said, "I can't right now, I'm working on a paper." All that time and money, trying to find a religious solution to my search for something authentic. I wouldn't get those years back, but I could do something about the years to come.

A church in Springfield, Massachusetts, had an opening for an associate minister. I wasn't sure I wanted it, but I needed to find out. I submitted my profile, and in March, I accepted their offer. With Peter at his church in Easthampton, we could be together again. Women in ministry were beginning to be tolerated, though not enthusiastically accepted. I was hired to develop their Christian Education program, as well as to preach every four to six weeks. I would also assume the duties of pastoral leadership when the senior minister was away. I looked at the curricula for Christian Education and didn't like any of them. Having children divided into age-related groups, sit in a circle, read from the Bible, and color in coloring books made me think of my own Sunday school days. Where was the excitement? Couldn't some of the Bible stories be made more interesting and accessible to children? Furthermore, asking volunteers to teach something they probably didn't know much about felt completely wrong and unfair. So I did something about it.

With the help of other church members, we created learning centers that changed every six weeks and involved people of all ages. The adults offered their talents to create experiences and activities based on biblical stories, and the children got to choose the center they were most interested in, regardless of their age. It gave adults and children a chance to establish relationships that might not otherwise have happened. Peter was using the same format in his church in Easthampton, so we frequently collaborated. We never had difficulty finding people to help, because they were drawing on their own interests like carpentry, art, music, or storytelling. I was pleased with the programming, but personally and spiritually, I still wasn't fulfilled.

Each week, ministers in our area met to explore resources for Sunday worship. At my first-ever gathering in my new role, I nervously entered the room and took a seat across from a man with dark-rimmed glasses, bushy eyebrows, and a roguish smile. Rich was serving a prestigious church in the center of Springfield, which had a reputation for hiring tall, white men to fill the pulpit. Before the meeting got under way, someone asked him to tell the story of his hiring process. It was well known that, until recently, only men could be deacons in this historic New England church, and their dress code was tuxedos. In his strong East Boston accent, he described his second interview with the search committee. Toward the end of the meeting, a woman asked him about the use of inclusive language, a hot-button issue in church circles in the 1980s. Was God mother, or was God father? He tried several times to explain that we need to think metaphorically when dealing with religious language. But she continued to press him until he blurted out, "I didn't know God had genitals!"

Rich continued regaling us with stories. "That pulpit wasn't built for short guys like me," he began. "I stood at the lectern in my clerical attire, looking like a bishop ready to preach my first sermon, but no one knew I was there! After some scurrying around, one of the deacons appeared with a footstool. Now visible to the congregation, I looked out and said, 'Oh, there you are!'"

This clearly was a minister who was not afraid to speak about his own vulnerability, which made me think he might be able to meet me in mine. His irreverent reverence appealed to me. The following Thursday morning, I knocked on the door to his office. That was the beginning of our monthly meetings.

It was so simple. He listened. He didn't judge. I took my dreams to him and talked about the things I had never shared with anyone: my grief, my despair, my shame, my terror of separation and nothingness, my fear of abandonment and death. He didn't challenge me, and he didn't tell me everything would be fine. He simply asked thoughtful questions, leading me deeper into those things I was ashamed to talk about. He affirmed my struggle and helped me find the courage to stop hiding.

Three months after I began seeing Rich, I noticed that my skin was clear.

Chapter 10

Erik didn't come out to us until he was a senior in college, but he'd known he was gay from the time he was 16. Peter and I had our hunches. He was an active child who loved to climb trees and scale rock faces. But when I tried to steer him toward traditionally boyish things like baseball, he just stood in the outfield daydreaming. When he wanted a Baby Alive doll, I bought him an electric train.

I grew up in a world where boys were supposed to love girls and girls were supposed to love boys. Anything else was considered shameful and unnatural. Homosexuality was considered a choice by many experts; some said it was "caused" by overly protective mothers. It was even listed as a pathology in the *Diagnostic and Statistical Manual of Mental Disorders*. When Erik got a little older, I told him it was normal to have feelings for boys as a teenager. Perhaps he just hadn't found the right girl. I never said it might mean he was gay, because I was hoping that the right girl *would* come along. Gay kids were bullied. They were teased and called fags. What kind of life would that be for him? I couldn't bear the thought of him being hurt.

I sought a therapist to help me sort out my feelings, and she told me I was homophobic. That came at me as an accusation. I didn't need to be made to feel any worse about my views.

When AIDS appeared, it wasn't ridicule that scared me. It was the sheer terror that Erik would get sick and die. I'd hide in my office poring over any materials I could get my hands on about how it was transmitted. This was the 1980s, when there was no cure and only experimental treatments. I took a chance once and confided in a good friend who was a Christian Scientist. She told me he could be healed. I knew then it wasn't safe to explore my fears with anyone. I wondered, outside of Peter, who I *could* trust. The answer was no one. I was now holding the biggest secret of my life.

I saw pictures of young men dying alone because their families had rejected them and wouldn't support them. I had to make sure that Erik was protected. Little did we suspect that this boy we feared would be bullied would someday travel the world working in the deep trenches of fighting racism and injustice.

Six months after I began my ministry in Springfield, I was asked by the senior minister of the church to take one of the two Easter services. The scripture for the day told the story of Mary Magdalene and the other Mary carrying burial spices to the tomb in the early morning following the crucifixion of Jesus. When they arrived, they found the stone protecting the tomb had been rolled away.

This passage made me think about the secrets so many of us carry because we're afraid or ashamed. We're blocked by the stones that guard them. The opportunity was clear. Move the stones. Take a look inside that dark place. Explore it. But I couldn't challenge the congregation to do that unless I started with myself. I got to work trying to figure out how to use my own experience as a way of undergirding the message of the story. All my life I'd been hiding the things that made me feel uncomfortable: my childhood fears, my mother's illness, my phobias, Erik's sexuality. I was the Queen of Stones. I knew I couldn't be silent anymore.

While I was now comfortable with Erik's sexuality, it had hadn't been easy for me. First, I had to get over all the cultural norms that clouded my thinking. Could he have a full life, would he be happy? Then I had to arrest the fear that being gay meant living in constant danger. Finally, I had to face my concern about what other people thought—and my shame. I was not proud of how I had once felt, but I *was* proud that I was able to overcome those feelings.

I wanted to share my struggles. With Erik's consent, it was time for the Queen of Stones to come clean. And if that meant the congregation would ask for my resignation, so be it.

On Easter morning, I stepped through the door leading into the chancel and into a din. Days before, the senior minister and I had drawn straws to see who would do the early service and who would do the 11:00. I drew the early one. I knew what that meant: babies crying and children squirming while I told one of the most intimate stories of our family's life. And just as I thought, kids were squabbling and squealing, and parents were shushing. My head buzzed. And then I looked out and saw Erik and Tim. Erik was no churchgoer, but he'd flown in from Washington, D.C., where he was working with AIDS patients.

As I stood at the pulpit, I recounted the story of the Marys at the tomb. I read from the Scriptures, lingering on the idea of facing our fears and rolling back our personal barriers in order to let in the light. And then with my sons bearing witness, I told the congregation the story of Erik's coming out. Suddenly the place grew silent. The babies stopped crying, the children were quiet, the parents were still.

After the service, as I stood greeting people at the entry, several told me they were sorry for my "problem," but just as many took me by the hand and said, "Thank you. You've just told my story."

I spoke my truth, and it did not destroy me.

If I was going to continue in church ministry, I needed to initiate the ordination process. The first step was an examination with the Church and Ministry Committee, a ten-person group of clergy and lay members. I had to present a paper explaining my theology, as well as what brought me to seek ordination.

The meeting was held in the back of the United Church of Christ in Amherst. I scoped out the room where the committee would meet with me. It appeared to be a Sunday school classroom. As I peered through the window, someone gave me a signal that they weren't quite ready. Clearly, they were discussing what they were going to do with me and to me. Suddenly, this didn't seem like such a good idea. Did I really want to go through with this? There was still time to change my mind: *Sorry. I made a mistake. I am not cut out for this. I'll just be on my way. Thanks anyway.* But just then the door opened, and a pleasant-looking older man ushered me in to take my place in their circle of metal chairs. Once I was seated, they welcomed me and introduced themselves. The chair of the committee explained the process: I would read or talk about my paper, followed by a period of questioning. I adjusted myself in my chair and took a deep breath. No backing out now.

I thought that presenting the theological section of my paper would be the challenge, but I breezed through it, surprisingly re-laxed. Then came the second section: my personal faith journey. My throat tightened. I began to tell the story of my mother's faith and death. But as soon as I started to speak, I had to pause, trying to push back the feelings that were about to explode. It didn't work. For ten long minutes, I sat in this circle of people who were there to determine whether I was qualified for ordination and cried so hard I was shaking. I was fifty years old. It had been 25 years since my mother's death, and the grief and denial that had been buried for so long poured out of me.

When the meeting was over, the minister who was to guide me through the next steps leading to ordination escorted me out. I could barely look at her because I knew I had made a fool of myself. As we walked from the room, I heard her say, "You are exactly what we need. Remember, Aaron had to speak for Moses because he stuttered; he couldn't speak." *Wait a minute,* I thought. *She must be trying to make me feel better. I couldn't possibly be what anyone needs.*

Four months following my meeting, I was sitting in a pew of the Easthampton Congregational Church about to deliver the same paper I'd given to the committee, except this time to a church filled with 150 people. "The Hampshire Association of the United Church of Christ has called this Ecclesiastical Council to order for the purpose of determining the fitness of Eleanor Mercer for ordained ministry in the UCC. The required documents have been received and are in order. Eleanor, will you please come forward."

Peter was in the front row. His presence was comforting, but it also made me nervous. I didn't want to embarrass him. I had confidence in my ability as a speaker. I did not, however, have confidence in my ability to answer questions. When I couldn't write things out ahead of time, I really was like Moses needing an Aaron.

Rather than reading through the entire paper, I highlighted parts of it. When I finished, the moderator opened up the council for questions. The first one came: "Tell us about your doctrine of free will." Was I supposed to have one? Panicking, I said to myself, *Well, Ellie, you either need to leave right now or at least make some sound. Something has to come out of your mouth.* Out came the words. I don't know where they came from. They just flowed out of me. Each time a question was posed, I paused—*Oh no. How do I answer that?*—and proceeded to speak. This went on for over an hour.

When the session ended, I was drained. Peter and I were asked to leave the sanctuary while the members of the association voted. I didn't know how I was going to face him. I just wanted to get out of there. As we exited through the back of the church, I looked at him and said, "Peter, I'm so sorry. What if they ask you to hand in your resignation because of me?" Peter is not an effusive man. He never offers a compliment unless he really means it. I could tell by the expression on his face he didn't know what I meant.

"El, I don't know what you're talking about. I couldn't have answered those questions as well as you did."

Ten minutes later, the moderator opened the sanctuary door to the roar of applause.

Chapter 11

Peter's wish had always been to return to Maine, so three years later, when I was offered a position as an associate minister in a large church in Portland, I accepted it. I didn't want to be separated from him again, and this time he would be four hours away rather than thirty minutes. I also couldn't imagine living alone. But Peter had sacrificed so much for me. This job meant a path back to the place he'd left on my behalf. I wanted to do this for him and trusted he would follow as soon as he could.

My primary responsibility was, again, in Christian Education with preaching opportunities every six weeks. But my image of someone with "Rev." in front of her name was a person unwavering in her faith. That was not me. I was a seeker. I saw my choice to continue in ministry as a way to immerse myself in a spiritual quest *with* others, not necessarily to lead them. On Sunday mornings, when I put on my robe and my stole, part of me felt like I was playing a role. I wanted to meet the expectations of my call to this church. I just wasn't sure I could do it. I told only my closest friends about my agoraphobia, my doubts, my fears. Yet, I knew it was those feelings and experiences that were propelling me forward on my search.

Peter came to Maine on Thursdays and drove back to Easthampton on Saturdays. It was like we were dating again. I hated standing at the living room window of my rented apartment watching him walk down the street, get in his car, and drive away. I missed him and our children, who were living and working in New York. Although I was busy, it didn't take away the loneliness of being separated from my family.

Two or three times a year, Bill Gregory, the church's senior minister, offered a series based on his book *Living Faith*. The participants were invited to explore *experiences* of God, rather than *ideas* about God. Some members of the group were trying to come to grips with misconceptions and illusions about the religious life, especially Christianity. I was one of them. Around this time, two friends from the church, Susan Doughty and Meredith Jordan, and I designed a women's series called "Deepening in the Spirit." Susan was a nurse practitioner and Meredith was a therapist. It was the 1990s. Women were still trying to find their own voices. Many who joined us had left churches because of a patriarchal system that didn't include them. We read poetry, journaled, passed a talking piece, and shared our stories. We trusted each other, and that trust allowed us to speak openly and truthfully. "I hear myself saying things about myself that I didn't know were there," one woman said. This was the ministry I wanted to pursue.

Something inside of me was shifting. I wanted to do more group work. I didn't want the focus of my ministry be Christian Education anymore. I never did. But then what? One night, I dreamed I stood at the head of a table where I was facilitating a group of a dozen women. I was wearing my white robe. One of the participants asked me what I wore under it on Sunday mornings, and I replied, "That's anybody's guess." In fact, I was wearing nothing under it. I knew I could not go on living like an imposter.

I needed a therapist and a spiritual guide and found one in Michael Dwinell, an Episcopal priest who had left the church to form his own practice in spiritual formation. Michael's brochure advertised his focus as "exploring all the risky and difficult things one might discover about oneself and about God." He'd graduated from an elite private school near Boston and majored in Islamic Studies at Harvard. He allowed as how everything I had ever been taught to believe was "bullshit."

I began seeing him twice a month.

I also made an appointment with an astrologer. I knew some in the church viewed astrology as heretical and others considered it bunk, but I was willing to try anything to help me figure out my next steps. Besides, what did I have to lose?

It was a beautiful fall day as I drove up the Maine coast for my appointment. I'm not sure what I expected. Gypsy scarves and tarot cards? Instead, I was greeted by an attractive woman in her early fifties who offered me tea before leading me into a sunny office with windows looking out onto a meadow.

"I've never seen a chart quite like this," she said, as she spread the document out between us. She pointed out how the blue lines far outnumbered red lines. "There isn't much here except someone whose relational energy is paramount. I would call it strong Mother-Earth energy. It's all heart and no mind."

I hated to admit it, but the profile fit. I always knew that strong relational side of me did not hold much value in the world's eyes. All heart. No head. Did that mean I didn't have a brain? Furthermore,

Mother-Earth energy wasn't exactly a formula for gainful employment.

Eventually, Peter was called to a church in southern Maine. The first morning we were back together, I looked out the dining room window of the parsonage. The sun was just coming up. It felt good to be in the same place again. But I was restless.

I left my position as associate minister with no real plan. I needed an income, so I accepted a part-time position as the Christian Education minister in the church Peter was serving. Once again, I was creating learning centers. But the position gave me a chance to work on forming a nonprofit organization with Meredith that focused on an examination of the demands and rewards of a spiritual life.

At this time, many people were breaking away from the churches they grew up in, with no place to go. Drawing from our experience with "Deepening in the Spirit," we created a space where people could explore inner experiences as well as belief systems. We never had trouble filling our groups. It was good work, and I knew there was no turning back. I was starting to find my true calling: to listen, rather than teach and preach.

On January 15, 2000 I was about to leave for the office when the phone rang. My stepsister was visiting my father and her mother at their winter home in Florida. "We can't wake your father up," I heard her say. Her words made no sense to me. What did she mean by "we can't wake him up?" In his weekly phone call to me a few days earlier, he had mentioned that he was seeing double and was planning to make an appointment with his optometrist. But it never occurred to me that anything was wrong other than perhaps a need for glasses.

And then she said that he had been unresponsive since two a.m. He was still at home and no one had called an ambulance!

I called Jeannie. We had to get down there right away, and that meant getting on a plane. I hadn't been on one since my trip to Bermuda, and I wasn't sure how I was going to do it now. But I didn't have the luxury of choosing. There was only one way there, and that way had wings.

The next day, I met Jeannie at her house in Boxford, and her Peter drove us to the airport. Perry had tried to get a flight out to join us, but she was traveling for her job and couldn't make connections work.

By the time we arrived in Florida, our father was in the hospital, unconscious. As the nurse took us to his room, she explained that his kidneys were failing and that he wouldn't survive much longer. The only sound was the whooshing of the oxygen mask as this strong athletic man, known affectionately to his students as "The Bull," lay completely helpless and alone. Frieda and Susan had chosen not to come to the hospital because watching him die was too difficult.

We pulled up chairs next to his bed, held his hands, and sat in silence, not knowing what to say. He was the patriarch of our family, priding himself on taking care of us. Now we were here to take care of him. Finally, Jeannie said, "Dad, Ellie and I are here." We wanted him to hear our voices and feel our touch so he would know he was not alone.

I thanked him for all the times he had rubbed my back with his strong hand in the middle of the night to help me breathe. And for the times he had taken me out in the car to see if a change in the air would help. I wondered if he knew how much I loved him. Had I ever used those words?

Somehow, Jeannie had had the presence of mind while she was packing to grab a cassette player, along with a tape of his last alumni glee club concert. Every June, twenty to thirty men who had once sung in his glee club gathered on alumni weekend for a performance in the chapel. This event was a highlight of my father's year. We plugged in the cassette and put in the tape. The music started.

I could just see him standing in front of those men, conducting, arms waving, exultant as the chorus sang "The Senior Song." This was sung only at graduation, as the seniors threw their caps in the air and left the campus for their next chapter. Through tears, Jeannie and I sang along with his "boys."

Strangers once we came to dwell together.
Sons of the Governors tried and true.
Now we're bound by ties that cannot sever, all our whole lives through…
Gather closer hand to hand. The time has come when we must part…

After sitting with him for several hours, we went to a nearby motel to get a few hours of sleep. At three a.m. the phone rang. Jeannie scrambled to find it. Her tears said it all. Ninety-five years. Where did they go? Suddenly, time had no meaning. All those years crunched into one. He was gone.

A nor'easter was heading toward Boston. My worry about my father overrode my fear of flying on the way down. But now I had to face flying into a severe winter storm. How was I ever going to do that? Glued to the Weather Channel, I actually considered letting Jeannie go ahead while I stayed at my father's and Frieda's house until the storm passed. But I was breathing, and Jeannie and I were together.

The next day, the plane took off with both of us on it and was soon in the clouds, that formless void. And it was not dark. It was light. Under my breath I said, "Arthur, you and I are on this flight together." I knew I was not alone.

When I got home, a friend called and told me the blizzard had a name: Arthur.

Chapter 12

The following August, I was on my way home from lunch with friends when I spotted thick dark smoke ahead in the direction of our church. I got within a few blocks of what was clearly a huge fire. Roadblocks had been set up, and policemen were not allowing anyone to pass. I rolled down my window and yelled out to the cop, "Is it the church?"

I'd recently been worrying about Peter. His kidneys, which were already compromised, were beginning to show signs of further deterioration. During dinner the night before, he had told two close friends that he didn't have the energy to continue full-time ministry and was planning to announce his retirement. But now, all that seemed insignificant. This was here and now. I had to get to him.

The cop was frantically directing traffic away from the scene and barked at me. "Yes, now get going!"

"But I think my husband is in that building. I have to get down there!" I screamed.

"I don't care!" he yelled. "You're not driving beyond this point." It took every bit of self-control to not scream back at him, *Who the hell are you to tell me I can't go down there?*

I don't remember where I left the car. I just remember I couldn't run fast enough toward the site. When I got there, flames had already engulfed the church. A crowd had gathered. Several people came running toward me. "Don't worry, Ellie. Peter's OK. He's right over there."

He was staring helplessly at the inferno. Trying to catch my breath, I took his hand and pummeled him with questions. "Can they save anything? How did you get out? Were you the only one in the building?" I wanted to know everything at once.

Stunned, he related the series of events. He never took his eyes off the flames as he explained that the newly installed alarm system had gone off, indicating there was a fire in the sanctuary. "I left my office to check it out, never expecting that it was anything but a false alarm. I walked down the center aisle and ahead, I could see flames about to break through the narthex door. I ran back to my office, grabbed my Day-Timer, and left the building. The fire trucks were already here."

Thirty-three years of his ministry went up in smoke: biblical commentaries, years of sermons, books. Nothing was left, not even what he needed to perform the three weddings scheduled for the weekend. But I knew he would find a place and a way to do them. And he would never reveal his level of fatigue.

That night, hundreds of us gathered around the smoldering ashes. We watched as the steeple collapsed into a gigantic pile of rubble, the sound thundering through our bodies. In eight hours, this historic church built in 1863 was gone. All that was left was the Paul Revere bell and memories of generations of baptisms, funerals, and weddings.

The local high school offered their auditorium for services on Sunday mornings. The parsonage became the church office until a mobile unit was put on the site. Peter's decision to retire was delayed for two years. There was no way the congregation could do a search for a minister while they were involved in designing and building a new church. I was needed to help with ministerial responsibilities. My work with Meredith came to an end. Peter's health did not improve.

One year later, on my way home from breakfast with a friend, I decided to swing by the trailer to check in with the church secretary. I was doing most of my work at home. I breezed into the office like it was any other day.

"You don't know what's happening, do you?" Sharon was looking at me, shocked. She couldn't believe I was unaware of the news. "A plane has just flown into the World Trade Center. All flights over the U.S. have been cancelled, and the ones that are still in the air are being rerouted to Canada," she said.

My whole body stiffened. I couldn't move. *Our boys…where were they?* Just then Peter walked into the office.

"Where are Tim and Erik?" I shrieked, as though he should have the answer. Both of them worked in Manhattan. Erik lived in SoHo— too close to the World Trade Center.

"I've tried to call them, but all the phone lines are jammed. Let's assume they're safe until we have more information." Peter was always rational in a crisis. I was not.

"Assume they're safe? How can you say that?"

A church member came in with the news that another plane had crashed into the Pentagon. I needed to do something, and I didn't know what. I was stuck in this office not knowing whether our children were dead or alive. I tried to slow down the thoughts in my head. I paced back and forth. And then the phone rang. It was Perry.

"El, I think Seth was on the flight that just crashed into the World Trade Center. He's in New York, and I'm almost sure that's the flight he was booked on."

She was on the other side of the country, thinking her son had been on that plane, and I was in Maine not knowing where our children were. We were living a parent's worst nightmare.

I kept trying Erik's and Tim's numbers. I had to reach my boys. I thought the sound of the busy signal would drive me mad. One interminable hour later, the phone rang again. I couldn't pick it up fast enough. The receiver felt like lead in my hands. It was Erik.

"I'm OK but it's chaos down here." He was frantically escorting kids from the homeless shelter he was managing to what he thought would be safety in Central Park. "I can't talk now, but I wanted you and Dad to know that I'm all right."

Why did he think Central Park was safe? That could be next. All of Manhattan could be next. Nothing about them being in New York City felt safe to me.

I wanted more information from him. I asked if he'd heard from Tim. He hadn't. Before I could ask any more questions, he cut me off. "I have to get twenty kids to safety. I'll call when I can."

It took another thirty minutes for Tim to reach us. He had an apartment in Brooklyn and had slept in because he wasn't due at work until later that day. A friend had called to make sure he knew what was going on.

"I'm up on the roof of my building. There's a huge hole in one of the towers. "Oh my God! Black smoke and fire are pouring out of it! I've got to go!"

A few minutes later he got through to us again. He'd gone downstairs to look at the news and then returned to the roof. His voice was shaky.

"The towers are gone. They've collapsed. And you know what that means." He paused trying to take it all in. "Thousands of people are trapped inside." I knew this was a tragedy of unimaginable proportions, but all I could focus on was my family.

Not long after, Perry called. Seth's travel agent had made a mistake on his departure time, and American Flight 11 took off without him. A fifteen-minute mistake! If he had not waited until the last minute to be driven to the airport, if he hadn't stayed up too late the night before, he would have been on that plane. That was too much to take in.

All three boys were accounted for, but that didn't mean they were safe. How did we know there weren't more attacks planned? I needed to do something to protect my children, but I felt helpless. I couldn't drive to New York. There was no way in or out of the city. And what would I do once I got there? How many thousands of people were dying? The only thing to do was stand guard. So I went home, placed myself in front of the TV in our family room, and watched the news for twenty-four hours. I watched, again and again, as the planes flew into the World Trade Center. All night I waited for the next attack, waiting for Erik, Tim, and Seth to die.

For weeks, I phoned Tim and Erik all the time because I was terrified that something was going to happen to them. I remained glued to the news. I couldn't focus on anything. Every time the phone rang, I jumped. I'd lived with immobilizing fear most of my life, and just as I had started to bring it under control, it came raging back. If I didn't do something, I was going to explode.

I'd spent plenty of time wrestling with spiritual challenges, but now I knew I had to do something that would challenge me physically. When a friend suggested participating in a four-day bike ride, a fundraiser for people with AIDS, I actually considered it. The prospect, of course, was ridiculous. All my life my asthma had kept me from playing sports. But recently, I'd been prescribed a drug that eliminated any symptoms. Furthermore, I was 62 and hadn't been on a bike since I was 12. Yet, I was desperate. It felt like the only way to exorcise my fear was to pound it out of me. I called Erik, who had done the ride the previous year. When I told him about my plan, he said, "Yes, El. Go for it! We'll do it together."

I began by taking baby steps. I joined a gym. At five a.m. on a chilly October morning, I walked into a spin class to find five rows of bikes. I chose one in the back. I was surrounded by confident and experienced cyclists, dressed in special shoes, tank tops, and biking shorts. Towels draped around their necks. I was in a T-shirt, jeans, and sneakers. The instructor saw me looking puzzled and came over to explain the drill. After she showed me how to change the tension on the bike, she turned out the lights, turned on the music, and got on her bike in the front. We started with warm-up exercises, and then the music got louder and faster. I could barely keep up as I panted my way through that first day. But I returned the next day, and then the day after that, until I was spinning four times a week. I was slow, but I was doing it.

In January, I had to go public with my plan. Up until this point, I'd only told Peter, Erik, and Tim. But now I had to sign up for the ride, which included raising money. I sent a letter out to family and friends asking for donations. As the checks came in, I convinced myself it was because no one believed I could actually pull this off. When I received $500 from my friend Nan, who's also asthmatic, I thought, *I bet she can't believe I'm doing this.* Yet, in a month, I raised over $3,000.

That spring, Peter and I stood in our driveway with my new 18-speed hybrid Trek. I was decked out in all my official riding gear— the same special shoes and bike shorts I'd seen people wearing my first day of spin class, except now I was one of them. I clipped into the pedals, mounted the bike, and started to wobble. I struggled to free my feet from the clips but couldn't and promptly tipped over. As I lay there, I waited for Peter to tell me I was crazy. Frankly, if he had—if anyone had—I would've said, "OK. I'm done." But Peter just let me get up on my own and didn't utter a word.

In addition to my spin classes, I now had to add 60- and 70-mile weekend training rides with a few cyclists to prepare for the ride. I labored up hills I couldn't have imagined cresting in my former life. There were times I wanted to quit, but I'd raised the money, invested the time, and bought the equipment. In other words, I was screwed.

On the appointed day, I joined 1,600 other cyclists at Bear Mountain in New York, ready to begin the 350-mile ride to Boston. It had been eight months since the start of my training, and I was as ready as I was ever going to be. Music pounded through enormous speakers. The bass throbbed in my ears. I was doing this with Erik by my side.

The music stopped, and then over the loudspeaker came a call to join hands, all 1,600 of us. I turned to the young man on my right. "How are you doing?" I asked.

"I'm terrified," he said, as his eyes filled with tears. He was 22 and fit. I was 62 and asthmatic, but we were going to be OK.

The starting gun fired, followed by an eerie silence. I could hear only the sound of people clipping into their pedals and the hum of the flywheels. I, too, pushed off, and I was on my way.

There were hills, traffic, and more hills. Each night we set up our tents, lined up for showers, and devoured meals carried in by volunteers. And each morning, before the sun rose, I could hear the soothing sound of revving motorcycles as Dykes on Bikes roared off to take their places at intersections to monitor traffic and keep us safe.

I was nervous about riding eight hours a day for four days, but I never lost my resolve, not even when I fell at a busy intersection in Connecticut and stopped traffic. I was there to finish, and I pushed on.

Four days later, we rode into Boston. Memorial Drive had been closed to all traffic. At the last pit stop, I took a breath. My butt was sore, my legs were bandaged from my fall, and I was ready to get off my bike. I checked messages on my cell phone. Erik had already finished. Now it was my turn. Only 15 miles to go.

As I finally pedaled into Government Center, I was exhausted, but I was breathing. And I wasn't last! I was somewhere in the middle. The scene was a wild sweaty blur. Crowds were screaming and cheering. Somewhere among them, Peter, Tim, Erik, and Jeannie— my family, waited for me.

As I crossed the finish line, I thought of my father. Maybe this was, in some miniscule way, what he had felt during the Parade of Nations in 1928, when he marched around the Olympic stadium in Amsterdam with athletes from all over the world. I could hear his laugh, see his smile, and feel his pride. I laughed, too, as I felt a weight lift from me. I'd done it.

Three years later, I would be on a plane to Italy—a trip I'd take just for fun, because I could. Bit by bit, I was shedding my fears.

Chapter 13

Four months after the AIDS ride, I was having lunch with a friend, a chaplain for a large New England hospice, who told me there was an opening for another chaplain. I had struggled with death and dying all my life, and now here was an opportunity to help people in their struggle. It's not that I wasn't afraid of what I would see, hear, feel, and even smell being in rooms with dying people and their families. I was. But this opportunity felt like a necessary step forward. I was sure this was the calling I'd been waiting for.

I rushed home and began work on my application. Within a few days, I was contacted for an interview. The clinical director invited me to join her in a conference room where we sat at the end of a long table. She paged through my file. "I see that your primary responsibility in the church was in Christian Education."

I bristled. "My responsibilities in the church also included working with people facing challenging life issues," I said, "including death and dying." I reminded her that hospital visitations, funerals, and memorial services were all part of my ministry. I told her about my group work, helping people go deeper in their spiritual journeys. Moreover, I knew the importance of being with people as they told their stories, shared memories and challenges, and sought spiritual comfort. "And," I added, "I've spent my life dealing with loss and my fear of it. That's not something I can work into a résumé." When I walked out of the interview, I was sure I'd been too forthright, too forceful, but six days later I was offered the position.

Shortly after I completed training and began seeing patients, I made a return visit to a man dying of cancer. I climbed the rickety stairs to his run-down tenement and joined his wife by his bedside. He'd been quiet during my two earlier visits, but today he wanted to talk. He described his experiences of childhood physical and sexual abuse in slow, deliberate language. When he paused, I waited. I didn't try to offer any words of comfort. What was there to say? When he finally finished, there was a long silence. His wife took his hand and said, "Please say a prayer for him."

I had no idea how to begin. I asked what she'd like me to pray for. She just wanted God's help and assurance that her husband would be OK. I took both their hands and managed to string some words together, but they meant nothing to me. What could a prayer do to ease a lifetime of pain?

I knocked on the door of Michael's office and took my seat on the worn-out couch with the frayed beige slipcover. At least I thought it was beige. It could easily have once been white. A wastepaper basket overflowed with trash. Michael, dressed in a roomy tunic, faced me from his leather swivel chair. Several gold bangle bracelets jangled on one arm, and a large cross around his neck rested on his sizeable frame. He was oversized in every way—his physical presence, his personality, his sense of humor, his ego, his intellect. He did not come across as a Harvard man from a prominent Boston family. Rather, he looked more like a hippie guru, and I trusted him. I told him about my visit.

"Michael. You know the worst part of this for me? It's that I don't believe anything I said."

"Well," he said, "trust your intuition. Pay attention to what's going on inside you. Words can get in the way."

I'd been on the job less than a year when I was asked if I could come see an actively dying patient. She'd been screaming for over twenty-four hours, and all efforts to comfort her had been unsuccessful. I wasn't sure what I could do if nothing else had worked, but I said of course I'd come. Although no one said so, I suspected I was asked to go there to give the other staff relief.

Before I went to the patient's room, I read her chart. She'd been active in a variety of social justice movements and was fairly well known for her efforts and accomplishments. As I approached her room, I could hear the screams. I was relieved to see that the hospice nurse was still there. We exchanged glances. She came over to where I was standing and told me she'd been there for nearly three hours with no change in the patient's condition. The facility nurse had just given the patient her scheduled dose of Ativan and morphine. They'd run out of options, she said, before leaving. That just left me.

I moved a chair over beside the bed, gently touched the patient's hand, and introduced myself. She screamed. I had no idea what to do, but then I remembered Michael's words: "Read the energy, whatever it is. Pay attention." I waited a few seconds, and then, gathering up my courage, I let out a scream. A couple of minutes went by, and she screamed again. So did I. Soon, I began to anticipate her screams and screamed with her. We seemed be forming a connection. In between screams, I affirmed her work and told her that I didn't blame her for screaming. I, too, wanted to scream at the injustice in the world. Suddenly, her screaming didn't seem so crazy.

I began to notice that her screams not only became less frequent, but also softer, until she stopped screaming altogether. For a while, I screamed for her. I screamed until my throat was raw. When I felt she was done, I left.

She died quietly several hours later.

Chapter 14

I stood on the sidewalk, waiting for Jeannie. We are both Virgos, and Virgos are characterized as being tidy, organized, methodical—and punctual. It always amused me that she was never on time, and I was always early. True to her not-so-Virgo nature, she pulled up in front of the church ten minutes late in her rusting blue Buick. I just smiled.

Now that I was working as a hospice chaplain, I had Sundays free. I'd suggested she and I meet in Newburyport, which would be halfway for each of us, go to her church, and then have lunch. Jeannie was considering taking the next steps to become a Christian Science practitioner. Although her path was different from mine, I believed in her. I thought attending church with her would be a gesture of support.

As she got out of the car, something didn't seem quite right. Her steps were hesitant, and her makeup, ordinarily carefully applied, was uneven and splotchy. She was wearing a bulky sweater, which was so unlike her usual tailored Talbots look. And she had a cough I didn't like the sound of. Still, it was good to see her. After a quick hug, we walked through the door into a small sanctuary.

Even though this was my first time inside a Christian Science church in over thirty years, everything was just as I remembered: the familiar white walls, the two lecterns for the two readers, the Bible passages interspersed with Mary Baker Eddy's writings. I sat rigid in my seat trying to focus; the readings meant nothing to me. But I was with Jeannie, and that's what mattered.

At lunch, she ordered a grilled cheese sandwich, telling me how thrilled she was to have an appetite, even though she only nibbled at her food when it came. I avoided the subject of church and focused on catching up on family news, but her cough kept distracting me. Finally, I said, "I know this is probably not helpful, but I wish you'd see a doctor about your cough."

"I'll be fine," she said. I knew better than to press any further. This was already an invasion into her strong faith. Besides, I never suspected anything more than bronchitis.

After my time with Jeannie, I started thinking about my mother again. It had been so long since her death, and there were so many questions left unanswered. In all these years, my sisters and I rarely talked with one another about it. I wanted to know if my memory of things matched theirs and decided to make a proposal. It was time to roll back another stone.

I sent off e-mails asking if they would be interested in sharing our experiences. Perry was in California, Jeannie in Massachusetts, and I was in Maine. I suggested that we meet for a weekend, where we would have uninterrupted time together. Most important, we might be able to tell each other how the events of 1964 and 1965 had impacted our lives and the lives of our families. Perry cast her vote. It was yes. I waited to hear from Jeannie.

Just before Christmas, Erik and Tim stopped at Jeannie's house on their way to Maine. Jeannie and Peter were hosting their annual Christmas gathering for forty neighborhood friends and families. Erik and Tim reported that Jeannie had to sit down periodically. This was not like her. If you were in her house, there was nothing that would keep her from doing everything she could to make you feel welcome. Resting would not be an option. They reassured me she otherwise looked fine.

The day after their visit, I received a response to my e-mail from Jeannie. *There are so many things I wish I had done differently that year,* she began, in reference to my query about those years. She said she knew something wasn't right when she went to visit our parents at Christmas. She told me she was concerned when our mother had to keep lying down, and our father kept asking if she was OK. And then she wrote: *I was too scared to ask, and since they never said anything, I thought they didn't want me to worry.* This was an all-too-familiar default response in my family. When she expressed her concern to her husband, he told her the truth he'd known since Thanksgiving.

She shared how hard the next three months were, especially since she lived so far away and couldn't visit as much as she wished. And then I came to a line that stopped me in my tracks. *I worked with Mrs. Kennedy and was so sure Mommy would be OK.*

Mrs. Kennedy. The same practitioner I'd worked with.

And there it was. My sisters and I had held the experience of our mother's illness to ourselves all our adult lives. I thought of the comfort and consolation we might have given to each other if only we'd had the courage to speak the truth. Instead, we each orbited our dying mother alone, isolated in our fear and grief.

Jeannie didn't mention getting together.

Two days later, one of Jeannie's daughters called. Something was very wrong with my sister. I said I'd be there the next day.

I walked into the wood-paneled den, where a fire burned in the fireplace and a small Christmas tree was set on the table in front of a picture window. Bunches of flowers hung from the beams of the ceiling. Jeannie dried her own flowers and used them in exquisite arrangements that she sometimes sold, although she was far more likely to give them as gifts. She was ridiculously generous. When she was in her fifties, she began offering piano lessons. If someone couldn't pay, she let it go. The children loved her because she always had treats for them. When she opened a candy store in the center of town, the children poured in after school and on weekends, often with no money. They quickly caught on to her good nature. That didn't matter to her. She wanted them to feel cared for. Eventually, she had to close because she was literally giving the store away.

Jeannie's house was the gathering place for our families, not just because it was cozy and warm, but because we all wanted to be around her. If we were troubled, she made us feel better. Her signature offering was chocolate chip cookies, ready at any moment to pop in the toaster oven. She always burned them, but no one cared. All we tasted was the love.

Jeannie was sitting in a worn blue leather chair. She was gaunt, her skin yellow, her cheeks hollow. I tried to hide my shock. *Pull yourself together*, I told myself. *Don't say anything about the way she looks. Just make believe this is like any other visit.* She was surrounded by her four children. Sarah and Virginia were taking turns giving her head massages. I thought back to our childhood when Jeannie and I had taken turns giving each other these same "head tickles." Shep and Mark, the family storytellers, worked at distracting us with memories from their childhood. My brother-in-law sat in a chair next to the fireplace, watching without saying a word. There was tension in the room, and I wondered if my presence was an intrusion. I wasn't sure my nieces and nephews wanted me there. I wasn't sure that *Jeannie* wanted me there.

But now everything started to add up: the bulky sweater she wore at our lunch to hide her weight loss. The cough. Her unsteadiness. My head swam. I hoped my face didn't reveal what I was feeling inside. *My God, I can't believe this is happening. This is my mother all over again.* The words spilled out of me. "Oh Jeannie, what can I do for you?"

She looked at me and without hesitation said, "Just see me as I really am." I knew what she meant—in Christian Science terms, to overlook what I saw and focus on who she was on the inside. But in truth, what she was asking of me was the most difficult request of all: Do nothing.

A few years earlier, she'd told me she was so firm in her faith that she would never let fear rule her thinking. Looking at her now, I tried hard to hold onto the memory of that conversation. The challenge was in trying to hide my own fear. I'd always imagined we would grow old together. She and Perry were my best friends. If Peter died before me, I would move closer to her. And now, all that was slipping away before my eyes. My sister was dying.

No one was prepared for this. Jeannie did not want medical intervention. Through the years, she had been clear about that. But her condition was worsening, and her Christian Science Practitioner wasn't available. A week later, on a cold January morning, my nephews bundled her in blankets and drove her to the hospital. They intended to bring her home as soon as her pain was under control.

My sister spent her last hours being cared for by a young inexperienced doctor. He bluntly told her she had cancer that had metastasized, which was the very thing the family had asked him not to do. My nephews never left her side. My nieces planned to join them in the morning, but they didn't get the chance. At four a.m. the phone woke me. My niece called to say that Jeannie was gone.

Chapter 15

Peter was in town at a meeting. I'd pleaded with him not to go. I suggested his labored breathing might be reason to cancel, but Peter doesn't take well to being told what to do. He dismissed his symptoms as asthma and left.

I sat with a book unopened in my lap. It had been three years since Jeannie's death, and I was still trying to come to terms with losing her. I kept reaching for the phone to call her, thinking of things I wanted to tell her. I wanted to share these feelings with Perry, but since Jeannie's death, a distance had sprung up between us. I wasn't sure why. We used to talk at least once a week. Now, it seemed that it was closer to once a month. I worried that might mean I was losing her, too. I feared the Eeyore in me was taking over and would drive people away when I needed them the most.

And I was worrying about Peter more than ever. Since his retirement a year before, his health had been deteriorating. His blood pressure was dangerously high, and his kidneys were failing. He'd recently had surgery to place two stents in one of his arteries. I couldn't even begin to fathom losing him, too.

My thoughts were startled by the phone. It was the nephrologist's office, calling to check on Peter. I didn't understand. He'd just been there earlier in the afternoon. Before I could respond, a woman's voice cut into our call.

"This is the operator." I wasn't sure I'd heard correctly. *The operator?* I thought operators were a thing of the past, and I certainly didn't know they could still break into private conversations. I was having trouble taking in any of this until I heard her say, "Will you accept a call from Marian Albee?"

With a crushing feeling in my chest, I said, "Yes." I knew what was happening before Marian, a friend attending the same meeting, said a word. "It's Peter, isn't it?"

She confirmed my fear. "He's on his way to the hospital in an ambulance. Gail and I will meet you there." Gail is a friend and a nurse who had recognized Peter's symptoms as more than asthma at the meeting they were all attending. She saw that he was slipping into unconsciousness.

I scrambled to get my coat.

When I got to the ER, Gail and Marian were waiting outside the trauma room. For five long hours, they kept me company until Peter was taken to cardiac ICU. Before he was transferred, the doctors allowed me to visit him for five minutes. He was in an induced coma, hooked up to IVs and scary-looking machines. His medical team was concerned because one of his pupils was enlarged, which was an indication of possible brain damage.

A doctor pulled me aside and asked if Peter and I had talked about orders not to resuscitate. "Are you telling me you think he's not going to make it?" I asked.

"We aren't sure."

I took a breath. "And if he does, are you suggesting that he might not be the same person who came in here?"

He nodded.

I was in freefall.

Friends came to the hospital every day as I waited for each bit of news about changes or complications. Tim and his fiancée, Casey, as well as Erik came from New York. Each day there was a new issue. First, it was pneumonia. Then he was taken for X-rays because the doctors couldn't figure out why he wasn't waking up. The specialists—cardiologists, neurologists, nephrologists—were neither encouraging nor discouraging. On Peter's third day in ICU, the cardiologist repeated what I'd already been told in the trauma room: Even if he survived, I should be prepared that the lack of oxygen might have caused brain damage, and he would probably be in rehab for weeks. The only thing that kept me going was the support and love from friends and family.

On the fourth day, Tim came striding toward me in the waiting room. "El, this may sound crazy, but didn't the doctors have trouble waking Dad up following his hernia operation a couple of years ago?"

It was hard to believe that no one had picked that up from his medical records, but maybe there was something to it. Tim shared this information with one of the nurses, and within hours the sedative was changed.

Two days later, Peter improved enough for the nurses to begin weaning him off the ventilator. He started writhing around in bed as he struggled to remove the constraints on his wrists. And slowly, he began to regain consciousness. Casey, Tim, Erik, and I held his hands and talked to him, letting him know we were there. We asked him if he knew where he was, but he couldn't speak. It was late when we left the hospital that night.

When we returned the next morning, we found him sitting in a chair looking out the window. True to his nature, he had defied the nurses' instructions not to get up without their help. As we crowded around the door to his ICU room staring at him, he casually turned to us and said, "What's wrong?"

We laughed. We cried. Our reactions annoyed him. Peter does not like big deals made of anything. He was still trying to orient himself and adjust to the news that he'd had a heart attack and that his kidneys had failed. In his haze, he had thought he was being held somewhere in an Asian prison camp. During the night, the nurses kept explaining to him that he was in the hospital, that he was not in prison and had not done something terrible as he feared. He had no memory of this or any of the events leading up to it. He'd just lost six days of his life.

A week later, he was discharged and began eighteen months of dialysis. As the weeks went on, it became clear he was a good candidate for a kidney transplant. There were two options: a cadaver kidney or a living donor. I knew right away my blood type eliminated me. We had a family meeting. Both boys insisted on being tested. Peter was resistant, saying he could not justify putting the kidney of a young person in his 68-year-old body. He said it was too risky to have Erik or Tim make such a sacrifice to prolong his life. Well, that was his opinion. We took a family vote. Three-to-one in favor. Peter deferred to our wishes.

The testing revealed Erik was a perfect match. It was a disappointment for Tim, who had hoped to be the donor. "I would have loved to be able to give part of myself to you, Dad," he said.

It took a year and a half for the transplant to take place. On the appointed day, Peter and Erik were taken to cubicles across from one another at Maine Medical Center, where the preparations for surgery began. Their vital signs were checked, their hospital bracelets were attached. A black X was drawn on Erik's body to mark the spot for surgery.

The anesthesiologists came in to talk with each of them about what they could expect. They would make sure Peter and Erik were comfortable. A few minutes later, the two surgeons made brief appearances. One would remove Erik's kidney, transport it to the team in the adjoining operating room where the other would place it in Peter.

At seven a.m., the nurses arrived in Erik's cubicle. "Are you ready?" they chirped as they helped him up onto a gurney and took him over to Peter to say goodbye. As I followed, I began to be filled with a sense of complete helplessness. *Goodbye? Are you kidding? Just like that?* When they rolled him out of Peter's room and down the hall, I had to suppress an urge to call out, *Stop! Bring him back. You can't have him,* but before I could, they turned the corner and disappeared with my child into the OR.

In the months prior to this moment, I'd treated the transplant like a tonsillectomy rather than a major event in all our lives. I had confidence in the medical expertise. But now, all the questions I'd neglected to ask when I had the chance flooded my brain. *What if something happens to his other kidney?* The doctors had assured me that both Peter and Erik would be fine. I trusted them, but now I wasn't sure. *This is not just about two kidneys, you know. This is about my husband and my son!* A few minutes later, they came and wheeled Peter into the adjoining operating room. There was no turning back. My worst fear—that I could lose them both—cascaded over me.

I went to the lobby of the hospital to wait. Two friends arrived with coffee and muffins to keep me company, but I couldn't eat. I sipped the coffee for something to do. Three hours later, the buzzer I had been given went off. Erik was back from surgery. The transplant doctor spent a couple of minutes with me explaining that everything had gone well. He told me Peter had received a great kidney. That was good news, but what about Erik? He was now minus a great kidney. Not only that, he was in excruciating pain.

Peter was taken to recovery a bit later. Unlike Erik, he was high on painkillers and lots of prednisone. I was thrilled to hear Peter using the bathroom. I hadn't realized what a comforting sound a man peeing could be. But at the same time, I was annoyed with his euphoria. Erik was feeling anything but euphoric. He declined narcotics because he didn't like the way they made him feel. That's when I learned that recovery for the donor is more difficult than for the recipient. Erik was quietly trying to treat his pain with Tylenol. He would never be able to take Ibuprofen again because he now had only one kidney. What else hadn't they told us?

For three days, I went back and forth between their two rooms. Erik seemed to prefer being left alone. I wanted to hover. Each day, Peter felt better. He would walk into Erik's room dragging all his equipment with him ready to spend time talking. Erik just wanted to sleep. *This is my body given for you* was no longer just a metaphor. Our son had literally given part of his body to save Peter's life.

I didn't know where to turn. Erik was sinking further into what felt like depression, and I was sinking with him. I was angry with myself for not getting more information about the consequences for the donor, angry at Peter for being so jubilant. How could I ever tell anyone I was anything but delighted by the outcome of this surgery?

Three days later, they both came home. Peter talked to friends on the phone, read the cards that arrived daily. Erik kept to himself. One afternoon, I joined him out on our porch. As I sat down beside him, I saw tears running down his face. My heart broke. I wanted to do something. Take his pain away. Protect him. But I didn't know how.

"I'm going out for an ice cream," he said, looking away from me. Not a beer, not a glass of wine, but an ice cream. My adult son suddenly became my little boy again. I asked if I could go with him, but he wanted to go alone. I watched him put on his jacket, walk down the driveway, and drive off without me. A week later, he returned to New York.

When I returned to work, the clinical director called me into her office. Clearly, I was unable to hide my despair.

"How do you think you're going to be present to dying patients and their families looking the way you do? Go home. You need to take care of yourself so you can take care of others. I'll see you when you're ready to come back."

That was an order, and I readily complied. I knew I shouldn't be there. I felt I had failed my son. I couldn't risk failing anyone else.

Chapter 16

Peter and I were sitting by the fire watching the evening news. We had just finished dinner. The snow was piling up outside our condo, and soon we would hear the clanging of the plow as the blade scraped the pavement pushing the snow to a drift at the end of our road. We were feeling smug about the fact that we wouldn't have to shovel. It was a perfect evening to be snowed in.

It had been two years since the transplant. Erik was managing well on his own, busy with work and soon to be married to Sandro, a wonderful man from Sardinia. Tim and Casey had moved to Maine so she could take a teaching job. Peter's health had stabilized. The plow clanged again. I took a sip of wine and went back to reading.

And that's when the phone rang. It was Rachael. "Auntie, can you come out here right away?" Rachael's usually calm voice was strained. I took a deep breath. "It looks like Perry is going to be admitted to Cedars-Sinai. You don't have to worry about any of the flight arrangements. We'll make them from here if you can just come."

Of course I would go.

It took a few minutes after I hung up for this news to sink in. Perry going to a doctor? To the hospital? Was she really going to agree to this? Perry, unlike Jeannie and our mother, was not a Christian Scientist. She claimed to be an atheist, although I think that was her way of saying she hated God and anything to do with organized religion. Perry grew up believing bad things disappeared if you just ignored them. She never went to the doctor. The only medical attention she ever received was when she was in her thirties. On a winter day, she had parked her car on an icy hill in Connecticut where she and her family lived. As she opened the driver's door to get out, the car slipped out of park and rolled over her. She was in traction in the hospital for three months. Friends came. They brought pizza and smuggled in wine, which the hospital staff pretended not to notice. Only Perry could treat something like that as a party.

Then I thought back to the night of the rehearsal dinner for Tim and Casey's wedding in August. The distance I'd felt between us after Jeannie's death had grown even deeper. I wasn't sure why, but when I tried to talk with her about it, she always told me I worried too much and assured me nothing was wrong. I suspected it wasn't much fun talking with me when I was so worried about Peter's health. While his new kidney was functioning well, he also had prostate cancer, diabetes, and congestive heart failure. I couldn't pretend everything was OK when it wasn't. There just wasn't a lot of laughter in me those days. The wedding was the first time in two years we'd seen each other.

When she arrived at the restaurant with her husband, Ron, she ran to the bathroom without even saying hello. "Per," I said as she emerged, "I love your hair!" She had allowed her natural color, now a beautiful white, to grow in. It was shorter than I remembered and not as flat on top. Perry rarely had her hair done by a professional; she cut it herself.

"Have you been to a stylist?" I asked in disbelief. She told me she'd recently gone to someone in Beverly Hills. I had no reason to doubt that. There wasn't a hint of the distance that had grown between us. In fact, she even suggested that she and I celebrate my upcoming 70th birthday together in France. It felt like old times.

The next day, she called and told me she was too sick to be at the wedding. "There was something wrong with the beef last night. It was undercooked," she said. No one else had mentioned undercooked beef, and no one else was sick. But she repeated it over and over again as though I needed to be convinced. They were leaving right after the wedding to visit friends in Connecticut before they flew back to Los Angeles. I was crushed.

Standing at the window, watching the snow come down, I began to put it together. Two years earlier, Erik had told me he'd noticed a dark spot growing on Perry's head. When he asked her about it, she went silent and refused to talk to him. The day of the wedding was windy, and the ceremony was outside. Her hair would've blown around and possibly expose something she didn't want us to see. Perry's hair needed to hide any evidence that might raise questions, and the wind would reveal the truth.

Rachael met me at LAX. Seth had arranged for a limousine to take Perry to an appointment with an oncologist. She had agreed to go on one condition: that they allow her to go there alone. She wanted no one with her, not even her husband. Her only companions were the driver of the limousine and a bottle of Pinot Grigio.

The plan was that Rachael and Seth would meet her when she arrived. They invited me to go to the appointment with them. I didn't think Perry even knew I was there, so I said no. This was a time for the three of them to be alone.

There was a coffee shop across the street from the medical building. I found a seat by a window and took out my knitting. An hour passed. I imagined the oncologist giving them news no one wanted to hear. I wondered how she was presenting it. What would happen if Perry refused to cooperate with whatever plan the doctor was laying out for her?

There was something comforting about being in the city with people rushing around and the steady stream of traffic creating a constant hum. It helped take my mind off the reason I was out there. Knit, purl, knit, purl. My hands worked back and forth as I tried to press down the words: *Not again. Not again. Not again.*

And then the text came from Rachael. "It's bad. She's being admitted to the hospital right away. Meet us outside."

As I crossed the street, I saw two people coming out of the medical building: a man and what appeared to be an elderly woman. It took me a moment to realize that it was Seth and Perry. The woman beside my nephew was not someone I recognized. She was dressed in baggy pants, a hat, and a scarf. Her clothes were too big for her—or rather, she was too small for her clothes. Seth had her arm as they slowly rounded the corner to his car.

I didn't want to alarm her, so I moved closer and quietly said, "Per, I'm right behind you."

She turned. "Oh, El, I am so glad you're here." She couldn't have weighed more than a hundred pounds. And the strong perfume she was wearing reminded me of the days when my father smoked his pipe to mask the odor of my mother's untreated cancer.

The admitting process at the nearby hospital took forever. We sat on thinly cushioned chairs, each of us trying to cover up our worry and our fear. Loud voices bounced around the waiting room with stories or gossip about families and friends, who had done what to whom, who had what illness, who was getting divorced. I wanted to yell out, "Could you all just be quiet?"

"Do you have a DNR or an advance directive?" asked the nurse once Perry was settled in a room, a totally foreign experience for her. She hadn't been in a hospital since her accident. I had been with hospice long enough to become used to these questions, but this was different. This was my sister, not a stranger. "Don't worry, Per. It's just a routine question. They're required to ask it." But I knew it was an end-of-life question.

Once the physical exam began, Perry asked me to leave. She didn't want me seeing any more than I had already seen, and I was happy to oblige. The world came to a standstill. Just when I felt things were getting back on track with my last remaining relative, she was being taken from us. Our trip to France dissolved like a dream.

I joined Seth outside her room. He was talking with a neurosurgeon, a friend who had come to offer him support. And while this doctor would not be involved in Perry's care, Seth was well connected. He would use all his resources to ensure she got the best treatment.

I stayed with Rachael at her home, but it was not an easy time. Not only was she dealing with her mother, but she had a new baby to tend to. Because she could not bring Bella to the hospital, a nanny came in each day to take care of her. She and I would leave their house around 9:00. While we waited in line at the Starbucks in the hospital, we tiptoed around our fears, not really wanting to give them voice.

Instead, we told stories about Perry. We laughed about her inability to tolerate silence. "Was she always like this?" Rach asked.

"Are you kidding?" I said. "She never stopped talking from the time she got up in the morning until she went to bed. I swear that as soon as she discovered words, they just piled up inside her and she had to release them. My mother, exhausted from listening, would ask her if she could please practice her *quietness*.

"Did she ever tell you the story about nearly being kicked out of church?" I asked.

"No. What was that?" laughed Rach.

"When Perry and her best friend, Helen, were around six or seven, they were sitting on either side of their mothers at the Episcopal Church we used to attend. They knew better than to let the girls sit beside each other. But that didn't stop Perry. True to form, she leaned forward in the middle of the service and deliberately caught Helen's eye. That's all it took. They tried to contain themselves, but it didn't work. A burst of laughter erupted, and the Reverend Daniel Boone had to stop his sermon and ask them to be quiet. Our mothers were mortified."

I thought of Perry's last visit to Maine. I told Rachael about how the two of us were on our deck drinking coffee, and I had to go to the bathroom. "I tried to interrupt," I said, "but there wasn't even enough space to tell her I was leaving. On the way up the stairs, I could still hear her voice carrying on without me. The birds and the trees were audience enough for her."

Rachael and I carried on with our routine for several days, but I started to worry that I was getting in the way, overstaying my welcome. And, of course, I was concerned about being away from Peter for too long. As much as I hated leaving, I knew I had to go home.

The following week, Perry was scheduled for surgery to remove the tumor on her head. It was going to be a delicate and challenging operation. That procedure would be followed by plastic surgery, which was even more delicate. Her doctors were encouraging, giving her hope that she might have a number of good years ahead. Perry was looking for ten, which her primary care doctor said was a possibility.

Her prior avoidance of medical care was replaced by a determination to participate in everything medicine had to offer. When the time came, the surgical team was able to remove most of the tumor, but not all of it. Still, we all had hope.

Once she returned home, we talked on the phone often. She never lost her sense of humor and quick wit. She talked openly about her disease and her gratitude for the doctors. Week after week, she had radiation treatments that required wearing a tight mesh mask over her face. She would never have hair again. Eating was difficult because her salivary glands were affected. Life after radiation was going to be different, she told me. The dream for all of us was that there *would* be life.

Maybe she and I could take that trip to France after all.

At the end of June, I went back to California for a visit. Perry was finished with radiation, and we planned to have time together in their home in Ventura. No doctors, no treatments. On the 45-minute drive from the airport to their house, I thought about how things between Perry and me seemed to be normal again. I was excited to see her.

Ron met me at the front door and took me into the living room, where Perry was sitting on the couch with her dogs curled up beside her. She was wearing a turban, a tie-dyed shirt, and loose pants, rather than her usual slim jeans. She was slouching to one side. "Oh, El," she said as we hugged each other. She looked fragile.

I sat down beside her and took in the magnificence of the place: the view of Los Angeles, the gardens, the patio, the swimming pool with its adjacent gazebo. She said she was dreaming of the day when she would be able to walk down there. But for the time being, she was suffering from a self-diagnosed "pinched nerve" and was unable to manage the steps.

On the second morning I was there, Perry woke up unable to move her legs. Our time together was now going to take place in the ICU at Cedars-Sinai. It was clear she was not going to be returning home anytime soon. I wanted to give Ron space, so I packed up my things and moved to a hotel close to the hospital. That night, I went with Perry while they did an MRI. She was scared. I was scared. It took one and a half hours. The news was not good.

Rachael, Ron, Seth, and I made sure she was never alone except at night. If Perry had had her way, the bed would have been covered with dogs and a stray cat or two, but animals were not allowed. Neither were flowers. So instead, we brought some of her other favorite things: shoes, jewelry, pocketbooks. Each gift seemed to give her brief moments of joy. But I suppose those moments were more for us than for her. We could pretend she might eventually use them.

On her fourth day at Cedars-Sinai, Perry's private-duty nurse, Pearl, Rachael, and I decided to give Perry a makeover. My sister's makeup, like her personality, was bold. She wore heavy black eyeliner and bright red lipstick. We suggested she try a look that toned things down a bit. No one really cared what her makeup looked like. This was just our way of trying to do what she couldn't do herself, put on her makeup, and for us to help kill time in a colorless, timeless space. This was not exactly my area of expertise, so my job was to open Perry's makeup bag and hand the proper instruments to the makeup artists. With a gentle touch, they applied moisturizer, followed by a beige foundation and then subtle shades of eyeliner and eye shadow. Their blush selection matched Perry's coloring, and the lipstick they chose was a subtle red. Ten minutes later, Rachael and Pearl had succeeded in delicately highlighting Perry's naturally beautiful features. We held up a mirror for her to see. She smiled.

On some days, Perry wanted to watch movies. One of Seth's assistants had wired up a system that allowed her to view anything she wanted. Her favorites were *Sleeping with the Enemy* and *The Shining*. She was only able to watch portions of them before she dozed off, which left Rachael, Pearl, and me sitting in chairs watching Jack Nicholson hatchet through a door while the machines beside us beeped away.

On other days we would just talk and reminisce. We told stories about the men we had loved. We reminded each other about how we used to laugh so hard that we had to move to separate rooms in order to breathe.

And then there was music. Singing helped us pass the time while Perry slept. She and I loved the folk music of the 1960s and '70s, especially Joni Mitchell, Joan Baez, Rita Coolidge, and Crystal Gale. One day Rachael, a professional jazz vocalist, began to sing "The Banks of the Ohio." Pearl and I joined in. The three of us took turns weaving in and out of different harmonies. I'd forgotten some of the words, but it didn't matter. It brought back a clear picture of Perry and me as teenagers sitting at the piano in our living room, a songbook open in front of us, singing that same song. Our voices blended. Sometimes my father accompanied us on his guitar. He was our most enthusiastic audience. Actually, our only audience.

The last day I was there, we started singing songs from *Oliver* and *The Sound of Music*. I smiled when I thought of Rachael's wedding rehearsal dinner. After too much wine, Perry and I decided to serenade Rachael and her husband-to-be with our signature song, "I Talked to the Trees" from *Paint Your Wagon*. When we came to the line *and they don't listen to me*, my brother-in-law cupped his hands around his mouth and called out, "Can you blame them?"

I know Perry wanted me to stay, and I was torn. I wasn't sure she would make it through the week, but I didn't want to be in the way of what should be Seth's, Ron's, and Rachael's time alone with her.

That night, as I made my way to the elevator in the hospital, I heard a harp. I stopped, stunned. A woman was playing Andrew Lloyd Webber's "Pie Jesu" from his *Requiem Mass*. This piece always made me cry. I don't know why. It just did. I couldn't move. The tears I had been holding back all this time streamed down my face.

I wanted the harpist to keep playing so I could release the devastation I felt. Over the years, I had wished Perry and I could keep singing, but we were never in the same place long enough for that to happen. And now the singing was over. No amount of praying or hoping was going to do anything to change the fact that the last member of my family was slipping away from me.

Merciful Jesus. Give them rest.

I hadn't been home in Maine a week when I found myself back at Logan Airport, sitting at the same gate, waiting for the same flight to LAX. Except this time, I was on my way to be with Perry in her last days. Rachael had called to say the time had come. The deal that Perry had with her primary care doctor was that he would inform her when they could do nothing more. He told her the tumors, now in her lungs, were spreading faster than they had imagined. The recommendation was that she go home and be comfortable. All the preparations were made for hospice.

I arrived at their house a few minutes before the ambulance. The hospice nurse was there with Ron. Everything was set up for her return. The living room was filled with medical supplies, and the hospital bed had been placed in front of the sliding glass doors leading out to a large deck with all her potted plants. I thought of my previous visit when she told me she couldn't wait until she could walk out that door, water the plants, and go down to the gazebo.

It was dark outside, and the thirteen steps down to the house were a challenge for the two female EMTs. Perry was on the gurney, wrapped tightly in white blankets. She didn't move or speak. The night nurse and Ron scurried around and collaborated on the instructions for her care. Perry slept for a couple of hours and then woke up saying in a weak voice that the ambulance ride was rough.

The next two days were spent adjusting to a new routine. The hospice nurse usually arrived around nine. Pearl continued to come. Rachael and Seth were there each day taking turns sitting by her bed. We occupied ourselves with small tasks. We watered her plants, prepared meals, did the dishes.

On the third morning, Perry asked for coffee and a donut. I found some bananas and used them to make banana bread. I soaked it in the coffee so that it was essentially mush. Ron tried to feed it to her, but she couldn't swallow.

In the evening, she requested her favorite drink, a Cape Codder, a mixture of vodka and cranberry juice. After checking with the nurse, Ron made sure she got whatever she wanted. He dipped a swab into the glass and placed it between her lips. She couldn't manage it.

Two days later, I sat on the barstool while she slept. Her blood pressure was low, and she seemed to be having trouble with words. At one point, she woke up and rasped, "El, could you take the Barbies out of the microwave?"

Not much made sense in that place and time, so I repeated, "Take the Barbies out of the microwave?" She laughed a weak laugh. I reassured her that I would take care of them. An hour later, she woke up again.

"El, am I dying?" When I didn't answer, she said, "I don't want to live this way."

My mind raced, searching for some words of comfort. I'd talked my way into my job as a hospice chaplain by asserting I knew how to be present for people, but I had nothing for my own sister. Finally, I said, "Per, you have a remarkable capacity for healing." My words hung in the air a moment

"I like hearing that," she said before drifting back to sleep.

In the late afternoon, Perry signaled that she was not comfortable. Ron asked that the nurse do whatever was needed for her comfort. Sitting by the side of her hospital bed, Ron told her the story of how they met, fell in love, and were married. The sound of his voice and the increased medication seemed to relax her. By 7:00 she was quiet.

We kept the large sliding glass door open so that it felt like we were outside while we were inside. The music of Tim Wheater, a New Age flautist and composer, played in the background. The night was beautiful; the air was cool. A crescent moon hung in the sky, with Venus shining beside it. Planes flew into LAX. The lights of the city sparkled.

Perry died at 8:18.

It was hard for me to leave, but Ron, Seth, and Rachael needed time alone, and I needed to get home. I packed my things and slept in a chair for five hours. My alarm went off at three a.m. for my flight back to Boston. On my way out, I stopped by the hospital bed and took one last look at our "Precie." I leaned down to her, so as not to wake Ron, who was sleeping and whispered, "How did this happen, Per? I was the least healthy of all three of us, and yet I'm the one still here. We were supposed to grow old together. Jeannie was the Mother Theresa. You were the Lucille Ball. And I was the Eeyore. You were supposed to outlive me."

The thing I had most feared all my life—losing my family—was now a reality.

When I boarded the plane and discovered I'd been assigned an aisle seat, my heart sank. The aisle felt too exposed. I longed to be next to the window, where it would've been easier to hide. I placed my luggage in the overhead bin, sat down, and closed my eyes, hoping to signal to anyone near me that I was not available for small talk. I didn't care where anyone was going or what they did for a living or how many children they had. I just wanted to be left alone.

Sitting on that plane, I told myself Perry was free from her pain, just as Jeannie and my mother were free of theirs. Although I hated that none of them sought the medical treatments that might have saved them, those were not my decisions to make. They chose their own paths that, like the enchanted castle of my youth, came with their own no-trespassing signs. All I could do was try to honor those choices and love them.

As the plane lifted above the clouds, I drew a deep breath. It was time to go home.

Epilogue

There's not a cloud in the sky. My weather app says it's a perfect 70 degrees with little or no humidity. My garden is as lush and full as it's ever been. And yet that sense of gloom starts to descend. I've had a dream that someone hurt my granddaughter's feelings. I could see her in a crowd, her back to me, crying. I wanted to call out to her, rescue her, but I couldn't get to her. I've been worried about Peter. He's been losing weight and having difficulty walking. Tim is still trying to deal with his grief over the death of his beloved wife, Casey, in a single-car accident three years earlier. I feel the weight on my chest and know I need to move.

I get out of bed and take a walk on a wooded trail near our condo. About halfway down, there's an area of sand where there's no growth—not something you'd expect to come across in the woods of Maine. This patch wouldn't appear to support life, but there—always in early June—I've seen a large turtle out here. This is where she lays her eggs. This seemingly barren place is, in fact, full of activity, the perfect environment in which to create new life.

It's been fifty-five years since my mother's death, sixteen years since Jeannie's death, and ten since Perry's. Each of these women I loved lived alone with their diseases and their demons. I often wonder how our lives would've been different if we'd been able to sit down with my mother and hear her story, read her poems, if we'd known about her breakdown, if we'd asked her to tell us why she chose the religion she chose. I wonder how our lives would have been different if, as women living a shared story in secret, we might have saved one another.

For much of my life, I was afraid to use my own voice, talk about my dreams. I was afraid to express my anxieties and my doubts, my own dark thoughts, my fear of dying—afraid to tell my own story. To pretend my mother wasn't ill, to pretend my son wasn't gay, to pretend I wasn't afraid of death and dying kept me from myself as well as others. But it's different now.

I have come to learn I have nothing *but* my experience. I don't know how to speak about God, but I do know how to listen, how to be present, how to feel, how to pay attention. And I do know that the fear of nothingness and abandonment and the urgency I feel when I am in that dark place is the cry that pushes me beyond the tomb of my own making into the light of something more.

I continue to be a member of a church, as well as an occasional participant in leading worship. I am able to let go of what I think I should be doing in favor of doing what I think I can offer. Furthermore, church offers me a chance to be part of a community of seekers. Although I am drawn to other practices and religious traditions, it is Christian tradition that I was born into, and that is what I continue to grapple with. But the stories in these timeless and ancient texts, no matter how old and no matter how difficult to understand, touch something inside me that speaks to what it means to be human:

darkness, light, jealousy, hatred, anger, love, justice, injustice, vulnerability. It's all there. I just need to be willing to look.

Like Eeyore, I still sometimes lose my tail. I never have a day when I don't worry. I watch the news about planes crashing. I worry about sickness, accidents that will take those I love from me. It's happened before. It will happen again. But I also am surrounded by people who love me, who laugh with me, share their stories with me—friends who are not afraid to explore their inner lives. My family, with its outrageous senses of humor, keeps the memories of Jeannie and Perry alive. At our family gatherings, we tell the same stories over and over again and laugh late into the evenings. No matter how many times they're repeated, they just get funnier. At these times, my shortness of breath is not caused by disease but by sheer joy of laughing, until I think there is no space in me for my next breath.

But there always is. There is always a next breath.

I watch the turtle work her way into the woods. I drink in all the life—seen and unseen—teeming around me. And then I remember I need to get moving so I can take my grandchildren to school.

The weight lifts. For now, everyone is fine, and that's enough.

Editor's Note

I have to confess when my friend Peter Mercer told me his wife, Ellie, wanted to talk to me about a book she was working on, I wasn't exactly enthused. Over the course of my career as a writer, editor, and educator, I've encountered countless people who want to discuss their writing. Everyone, it seems, has a novel or memoir tucked in a desk drawer, or the notion for one. They just need the right person to – well, you know – make the words magically appear and fall into the right place on the page for them. I figured Ellie and I would have a quick coffee, I'd open her eyes to the reality of book writing, and that would be the end of it.

Instead, she brightened at each obstacle and difficulty I said awaited her. She sat perched across from me sporting a silver asymmetrical bob, a flowing wool tunic, and a wristful of bangles that clanged each time she moved. "Yes!" she exclaimed, her big brown eyes lighting up. "That's exactly what I need!" She was not to be daunted – not even when I reviewed her manuscript-in-progress and told her much of it had to go. She was trying to address themes of personal darkness and denial, but what she had produced thus far was a theological thesis, replete with quotes, footnotes, Bible passages, poems, and perhaps scraps of discarded sermons. But beneath it all, I saw glimpses of a gifted writer who had a compelling story to tell. We just had to move all the academic gobbledygook out of the way.

In the 10 years that ensued, we worked together to excavate that story, even when we weren't entirely sure where we were headed. Ellie took the necessary time. Did the hard work. Courageous in life, equally courageous on the page, she was unflinching in exposing her struggles, even when it meant venturing into uncomfortable terrain.

During this process, she and I went from a cordial writer/editor relationship to a bond so close it was sometimes difficult to tell where the writing stopped and the editing began. That's not to say we co-wrote this book. These are Ellie's words. It was just that after hours and months and years of confidences and conversation, I could practically quote her back to herself. I just knew how to – well, yes – help her make the words appear and fall into the right place. But that's where my role ended. The magic is all hers.

Ellie Mercer is a retired United Church of Christ minister who spent the last ten years of her professional life as a hospice chaplain.